BRITAIN'S SEARCH FOR A ROLE

Britain's search for a role

LASLO V. BOYD
Assistant Professor of
Political Science,
University of Baltimore

SAXON HOUSE | LEXINGTON BOOKS

Published by
SAXON HOUSE, D. C. Heath Ltd.
Westmead, Farnborough, Hants., England

Jointly with
LEXINGTON BOOKS, D. C. Heath & Co.
Lexington, Mass., USA

ISBN   0 347 01103 9

Library of Congress Catalog Card Number 75-28613

Printed in Great Britain by
Robert MacLehose & Co. Ltd
Printers to the University of Glasgow

Contents

List of tables

List of figures

Preface

Britain's search for a role has attracted the attention of a large number of observers. Academicians, journalists, and public officials have commented on different aspects of what has become an increasingly complex issue. So, of course, has the British public. The commentators have, however, failed to reach a consensus.

Certainly it is a topic on which people have held strong views. Additionally, some of the observers have produced scholarship of a high level, of both an historical and a theoretical nature. Yet even after the British referendum of June 1975, the resolution of the issue remains unclear. Indeed, Britain may not find a role, or at least not in the traditional terms in which the idea has been discussed.

The research which resulted in this book started with the premise that Britain's search for a role was a matter of choice. That assumption is retained in the introductory chapter. Yet as the following chapters demonstrate, the search has been complicated by external factors over which Britain has had little control.

The objective of this study is to contribute to the understanding of a complex issue, in part by underscoring the complexity involved. I assume that readers will come equipped with prior knowledge and insights on this topic, and may be stimulated to continue the process of examination and analysis.

One final comment on my findings is necessary. The conclusions which I have presented are not particularly optimistic. Certainly the past record of British performance is not encouraging. I have tried to identify a range of possible developments in the future, but the idea that a major change in Britain's fate is in the offing must be considered with extreme caution. Projecting past trends into the future is a frequent error of social scientists, as some earlier studies of Britain show. The future may be different. If it is, however, it will be the result of adjustment, choice, and some luck, rather than the continuation of a trend, for the trends have been negative.

I would have preferred to come to a different set of conclusions. After doing research at Chatham House, or wandering through the Tate Gallery, or sitting on the terrace of Westminster watching the Thames flow by, it is hard not to be influenced, hard not to engage in wishful thinking. I have tried to minimise such factors, but the reader will have to judge whether the effort was a successful one.

I cannot blame anyone else for my conclusions. Certainly many others helped me along the way, and the results would have been impossible without their assistance. While absolving them of any responsibility, I do want to express my sincere appreciation for all the help I did receive. I obtained perspective as well as information in a series of interviews conducted primarily in London, Washington, and Brussels. The willingness of elected officials, civil servants, and other social scientists to share information was a highlight of my research. At the request of a number of the individuals, however, I will not identify them by name.

I do, however, want to mention several people specifically. Bob Pfaltzgraff sparked my interest in the topic initially, helped me with sources, contacts and information, and offered comments on a draft of the entire manuscript. Michael Hodges and Edward Moxon-Browne discussed over a number of years many of the ideas with me and gave me their own analysis of the British search. Alvin Rubinstein, in addition to encouraging me with the project, assisted with a travel grant from the Anspach Institute of the University of Pennsylvania.

I want to thank June Betz and Sharon Taylor for their work in typing the manuscript.

Finally, for assistance of every kind throughout the lengthy effort, I owe a special debt to my wife, Carolyn.

LVB
August 1975
Baltimore, Maryland

1 Introduction

Great Britain has lost an Empire and has not yet found a role. The attempt to play a separate power role, that is, a role apart from Europe, a role based on a 'special relationship' with the United States, a role based on being head of a 'Commonwealth' which has no political structure, or unity, or strength, and enjoys a fragile and precarious reality by means of the Sterling Area and preferences in the British market – this role is about played out (Dean Acheson, 5 December 1962).[1]

The search for an international role has been a major preoccupation of the British for many years. The decline from great power status had been recognised well before Dean Acheson's 'Britain is played out' speech. Indeed, despite the angry reaction to the Acheson speech,[2] the British have been quite introspective about their world standing.[3]

In 1948, Winston Churchill spoke of British foreign policy in terms of three interlinked circles: the Commonwealth, the United States, and a united Europe.[4] The order was significant. In subsequent years the British found that both their independent capability and the cohesiveness of the Commonwealth were declining. As the various efforts to build a united Europe progressed, the United Kingdom gave increased attention to that 'circle' of her foreign policy. At the same time, successive British governments pursued the alliance with the United States.

Attention to a world role is one matter. Making the decisions implied in a reordering of priorities has proved far more difficult. The historical observation that Britain has shifted from a global to an Atlantic emphasis in her international relations leaves unsettled the specific orientation within that area.

Two main alternatives have been seen. On the one hand, there is the 'special relationship' with the United States. Although this partnership has been deemed vital to both members since at least 1940, its form and saliency have varied enormously. The relationship has been studied from many different perspectives: as a traditional alliance,[5] as a case of political integration,[6] and as a unique phenomenon in international politics.[7]

The second alignment which the British have considered is participation in the European integration movement. Here, the British were reluctant initially, and at times actively opposed schemes for supranational organisations. Still, the need to come to some sort of accommodation with a united Western Europe

1

has always been clear to government leaders. A shift in approach was marked by the 1961 decision to apply for membership of the European Community. After years of on and off negotiations, Britain became a member of the Common Market in 1973. This third stage (of participation in supranational institutions) has not led to an end of the policy dispute within Britain on her international role. Both historical description[8] and analysis based on integration theory[9] have been used to examine Britain's relationship with the European Community.

Most comparative studies have advocated one or the other of the two alignments.[10] That the two are not entirely compatible has been widely recognised. The question has turned on the extent to which they are reconcilable. In January 1963 de Gaulle made it clear that for him the choice had to be either/or. His statement drew considerable attention to the dilemma facing Britain in determining her role. It is a dilemma which has not been dealt with easily.

A framework for analysis

The objective of this study is to examine the evolution of Britain's relationships with the United States and with the European Community. Moreover, since the two relationships interact, the areas in which they interact and how each has changed need to be assessed.

A difficulty arises as to how to compare two different kinds of relationships. A first step is to decide upon an organising framework. Rather than treat one portion of the subject as a dynamic process while continuing to think of other sectors as static factors which have a steady and constant impact on the process, it might be more useful to examine developments in international relations as processes, in terms of both their internal evolution and their interaction with other processes. Karl Kaiser has developed this approach using slightly different terms. He defines the term 'international subsystem' as

> a pattern of relations among basic units in world politics which exhibits a particular degree of regularity and intensity of relations as well as awareness of interdependence among the participating units.[11]

This definition, by focusing on a 'pattern of relations', permits going beyond the description of discrete events without becoming so abstract as to lose contact with reality. In addition, the notion of awareness suggests the requirement of consciousness within an international subsystem. That is, a member of an international subsystem is aware of interdependence and interaction with other members of the subsystem. While it is true that a number of different kinds of relations might meet this criterion, this in fact forms the basis for the examination of more than one kind of relationship at a time.

The Anglo-American alliance can therefore be thought of as an international subsystem. Similarly, the concept allows us to examine Britain's relationship to an integrating Western Europe both before and after she became an institutional part of the process. The existence of overlapping membership in these two subsystems makes the interaction between them quite explicit.[12]

These two alignments help to structure the international system.[13] As they interact and change, system transformation takes place. This study will focus on such developments from three perspectives. First, the role of Britain will be considered in terms of both her capabilities and her needs in the international system. Secondly, the internal evolution of each subsystem will be examined with regard to changes in the pattern and intensity of relations. Thirdly, the interaction of the two subsystems will be evaluated. This last concern will involve both observation of change and inference from the other two levels rather than the presentation of causal relationships. While it is assumed that the two subsystems interact, changes within each of them need not be directly correlated. A series of propositions on interaction are presented later in this chapter.

Any alignment is evaluated by its participants with respect to both actual and potential benefits. A major finding of Karl Deutsch was that all the cases of amalgamation which he studied were preceded by widespread expectation of joint regard for the participating units.[14] Value-maximising choices are not always available, however. On the one hand, access to potential benefits may require giving up present ones which are considered important. On the other hand, the evaluation of benefits from an alliance may differ from one functional sector to the next.

The first problem is the basis of political choice – the ordering of priorities. With regard to the second point, however, some analytical distinctions need to be made.

In studying integration, Joseph Nye has suggested a tripartite division.[15] He rejects Ernst Haas's contention that political and economic integration are on a continuum,[16] and instead argues that the relationship between them for particular cases must be empirically determined.[17] This position casts serious doubts on the neo-functionalist approach with its emphasis on the compelling logic of spillover, that is, the assumption that sector integration begets its own impetus toward extension. While there have always been doubters, this concept, in fact, has been the chief rationale of the European integration movement since 1955.

Both the hopes and disappointments of that movement have centred on the

3

applicability of some sort of functional theory to a real world situation. Setbacks within the political sector have led in turn to some theoretical reevaluation. Thus by 1967, Haas, the foremost advocate of this approach, reached the conclusion that 'integrative decisions based on high politics and basic commitment are undoubtedly more durable than decisions based on converging pragmatic expectations.'[18] Yet Haas still tended to blame the failure of spillover on a deviant case, that of de Gaulle. Kaiser has summed up the apprehension and uncertainty that have plagued both theorists and policy makers thus:

> We do not really know yet how the success of sector integration affects the area of high diplomacy or defense. Conversely, conflict in the area of 'high politics' can lead back into functional integration.[19]

These concepts from integration theory have application to this study. The examination here will be divided into three sectors: economic, military and political relations. No effort will be made to examine the social sector. Transnational factors which might be appropriate to social integration do not necessarily have a direct influence on the decisions or actions of national governments. That such factors may be background conditions for integration[20] does not mean that they are significant in interstate relations.

No assumption is made about a causal relationship among the three sectors. Rather each can be evaluated separately and then compared with the other two. The relationship among functional sectors is thus left for empirical determination.

The next step is to establish a standard for comparison of the two international subsystems. Britain, the focal point of this study and the point of overlap of the two subsystems, has particular identifiable reasons for seeking international alignments; that is, there are certain needs which the United Kingdom hopes to satisfy by her interaction with other international actors. It is possible to evaluate the ability of an alignment to respond to those needs. This latter responsiveness will be referred to in this study as 'importance'.

Thus, the 'importance' of alternative subsystems can be compared as can changes in the 'importance' of one subsystem over time. In application, however, the concept of 'importance' is not absolute. First, Britain's ability to choose her international partners is limited. As Britain cannot be considered the 'core power'[21] for either subsystem, assessments of her ability to contribute to the alignment become significant. In the example of the European Community, William Riker's assumption that control over admission to coalitions exists was clearly demonstrated by de Gaulle's two vetos of British applications.[22] Also, the solidarity of the 'special relationship' has been affected by American evaluations of Britain's capability. It is Britain who is searching for a role with no assurance of satisfaction; that is, coalition behaviour would seem to be determined by available rather than optimal options.

A second factor is more complicated. Although causal relationships have not been established, there is clearly interaction between different sectors. Interrelationships are crucial in two ways. First, as mentioned, the 'importance' of different subsystems may vary from one functional sector to the next. Secondly, the degree of commitment required for participation in a particular grouping may become a factor. For example, to obtain the economic benefits of a customs union, a nation might have to forgo certain military advantages associated with another alignment; that is, a nation may not be free to maximise its benefits in all sectors. The extent of this dilemma will depend on the nature of the subsystems involved.

For this study, two components of each sector's 'importance' are considered: policy and transactions. Attitudes and preferences are distinguishing characteristics of any international actor. As they become formalised by governments, they can be thought of as policy. Nations with identical or complementary policies have a basis for alignment.[23] This coincidence may be natural or it may be the result of deliberate choice by one of the participants.[24] Thus, agreements in policy can be empirically observed and taken as one measure of the condition of an international subsystem.[25]

Not every facet of policy need be considered. The notion of 'awareness' from the definition of international subsystem provides the key. The first step is to identify the *main* policy interests for Britain in each sector. At this stage, such a determination must rely on historical judgment based upon Britain's needs. Then an assessment is made of how each of these areas was treated within both of the subsystems. The focus is on the extent of agreement or of conflict exhibited. If a particular policy area was not dealt with to Britain's satisfaction, attention turns either to the seeking of an alternative partner in that policy area or to a shift in British policy.

Two additional aspects of policy interaction should be mentioned. While the emphasis is on *main* policy areas, other issues may become important. In the first place, policy stands may be taken or requested as a demonstration of commitment to an alignment. In addition, examples of special cooperation or of disagreement on certain issues may acquire a symbolic value which make them important in their own right.

The second 'importance' component, transactions, can be measured quantitatively. Yet both the selection of transaction factors and their evaluation depend on judgmental determinations. For a start, transactions correspond in the original definition of an international subsystem to 'regularity . . . of relations'; that is, the interaction between national units can be specified in terms of certain resource exchanges between them. Furthermore, the 'intensity of relations' can be evaluated by changes in transaction levels over time.

The analysis of transactions is a principal aspect of the theory of integration propounded by Karl Deutsch. For him, the links between societies are the primary focus of analysis. Yet these turn out to be social and economic ties. There is little explicit effort to relate them to the political choices which are made by government.[26] While the factors which Deutsch cites may well be associated with integration, they tell us little about the process.[27]

Thus Deutsch's use of transactions is inappropriate for this study. Transactions are here examined as a mechanism for meeting needs in the international system, not as indicators of background homogeneity or of communication. The needs are vital, not non-controversial. Although a variety of transactions will be presented, they may all be politically related.

Using the concept of 'importance' will avoid the problem encountered in integration studies of 'high' and 'low' politics. Nye's distinction is a useful reference point, however.

> 'High' politics is symbol-laden, emotive, and based on attitudes characterized by greater intensity and duration than 'low' politics which is consequently more susceptible to the rational calculation of benefits associated with economic problems.[28]

Integration theorists have placed great emphasis on this dichotomy. The neo-functionalist approach envisioned integration in 'low' politics spilling over with compelling logic into 'high' politics sectors. When de Gaulle stymied this progression in the European Economic Community, theoretical modifications were introduced. It has become apparent that the 'high–low' categorisation does not strictly correspond to a functional breakdown, such as political–economic.

The 'high–low' distinction was important because it related to the strategy of integration. In this study, all three sectors *may* involve 'high' politics. The starting assumption that the relations examined are considered significant by the participants enables attention to be focused on change and interaction. Thus, the full implications of political processes are considered. Indeed, the objective is to illuminate those processes rather than to demonstrate a particular conviction about them. The next step, then, is to present the procedure used.

6

Procedure

First, economic, military and political relations will be considered separately. In terms of capabilities, economic and military factors might be thought of as components of political status. Of course, this does not mean that relations in the political sector are determined completely by economic and military capabilities. A psychological perspective, which includes attitudes, perceptions and appearances or gestures, influences political relations in a way which often ignores material factors. For this reason, the analysis will proceed differently for political relations than for economic and military ones.

For the first two sectors, attention will be focused first on Britain's capability and how this changed. As has been suggested, this determination has a dual significance: firstly, the needs which Britain has wanted to satisfy through international arrangements can be specified; secondly, her ability to contribute to an international subsystem will become more evident. From a different perspective, these factors describe Britain's bargaining strength in the international system.

Then the condition of each of the international subsystems will be examined. The primary objective is to determine the 'importance' to Britain of each of the alignments. Thus patterns of both policy orientation and transactions will be considered.

The two subsystems will be evaluated both separately and relatively to each other. Attention will be focused on comparison and change. It will therefore be possible to observe how the two subsystems either coexisted or conflicted in terms of Britain's international position.

While the emphasis is on these two relationships as alternatives for Britain, the perspective of her partners cannot be ignored. There are two main determinations to be made. Was Britain seen as 'important' to her prospective partners? To what extent was Britain allowed to define the terms of interaction? That is, was Britain free to choose between the United States and the European Community in these sectors?

The political sector will be treated somewhat differently. The first portion will be concerned with negotiations between Britain and the European Community up to 1972. The fact that Britain applied for membership stands out as a significant political indicator for that period. This is followed by an examination of British participation in the European Community, including the effort to re-negotiate the terms of entry. This latter development suggests that, even after formal membership of the Common Market, the issue of Britain's role did not become moot.

Corresponding with this section will be an examination of the Anglo-American political community and of its evolution. Two facets are important here. First, what evidence is there that the two nations considered relations with each other to be 'special'? Secondly, how was the question of a British arrangement with the Common Market settled between the United States and Britain?

After the three sectors have been considered individually, an effort will be made to compare the trends and patterns in the two subsystems over all three sectors. This chapter will focus on both the substantive and the theoretical implications of the study. In addition to examining correlations between functional sectors, the overall interaction between the two subsystems will be explored. The basis for this evaluation is the following nine propositions. From the theoretical approaches set forth above, certain patterns of inter-action seem most likely to develop. Both the 'accuracy' of these propositions for this study and their implications for theory-building will be examined.

1.   Between 1958 and 1975 the 'importance' of the link with Europe[29] for Britain increased, while that of the connection with the United States decreased.

While this proposition is based largely on historical observation, the following propositions offer the possibility of being more precise. They all refer to the period 1958–75.

2.   The increase in 'importance' of Europe for Britain came first and most markedly in the economic sector.

Neo-functionalism suggests that integration proceeds first in a relatively non-controversial sector, the economic one. Even though this proposition has not been adopted for this study, its predictive ability is worth examining.

3.   In the military sector, the 'importance' of the United States remained well above that of Europe for the British.

This sector showed the least change in 'importance' levels. The military field is highly sensitive, an area of 'high' politics, and is not a likely sector for integration. In addition, the European Community has not made much progress in evolving into a defence community.

4.   The 'importance' of Europe for Britain in the political sector increased as her own economic and military capability decreased.

Europe was attractive as a 'core power' for Britain. The logic of Common Market membership became more compelling with the passage of time. Moreover, comparable opportunities for integration were not seen within the relationship with the United States.

5. As Britain's economic and military capability decreased, her bargaining ability, that is, her 'importance' to the United States and to the European Community, decreased.

If alliances are formed to meet real needs, Britain's ability to contribute to either American or European objectives would be seen as having diminished.

6. From proposition 5, the decline in 'importance' was greater with respect to the United States than to the European Community.

British economic and military capabilities represent a significantly larger contribution to a European than to an American total.

7. Overt demonstrations of commitment to Europe by the British were most intense during negotiations on membership of the European Community.

Proposition 7 involves an assessment of political strategy. It may be taken as a test of Britain's ability to bargain in the international system.

8. After Britain became a member of the European Community, transaction levels with Europe increased sharply, while the 'importance' of the American subsystem declined.

This proposition is an effort to assess the impact of institutions on international transactions.

9. Overlapping subsystems in which a superpower participates interact in such a way as to foster the formation of subsystems excluding the superpower.

Proposition 9 is taken from Karl Kaiser[30] and is stated in more general terms than the preceding propositions. It touches upon the idea of a European 'Third Force' and of an American–European split. This proposition also highlights the element of choice for Britain as the United States and Europe moved apart in many policy areas during this period.

Since trends do not lead to inevitable conclusions, the need arises to consider 'relatively accidental and historically unique factors'.[31] In line with this approach, the boundaries of the analytical period have been chosen to take into account historical events. Thus 1958 is selected as a starting point for the formal investigation of these relationships because that was the year in which the European Economic Community came into existence. This, in turn, intensified the pressure on British leaders to re-examine their relationship to the rest of Western Europe. The end-point is the British referendum on Common Market membership of June 1975. The vote, while perhaps not the final word on Britain's role, is certainly an explicit measure of choice.

The basic objective of this study is, then, to examine the evolution of Britain's relationships with the United States and with the European Community from 1958 to 1975. Both of these alignments fulfilled certain needs and were 'important' for the United Kingdom. Moreover, from the UK perspective, the interaction between these two relationships was not eliminated by attempts to join the Common Market nor, indeed, by the ultimate success of that endeavour. Rather, the patterns of relations within each of the sub-systems and the process of interaction between them were the basis of Britain's search for a role from 1958 to 1975.

Notes

[1] West Point (5 December 1962).

[2] Prime Minister Harold Macmillan retorted that Acheson had made the same miscalculation of Britain as had Philip of Spain, Louis XIV, Napoleon, the Kaiser and Hitler.

[3] For a discussion, see Uwe Kitzinger, 'Britain's Identity Crisis', *Journal of Common Market Studies*, vol. 6, no. 4 (June 1968).

[4] Speech to the 1948 Conservative Party Conference.

[5] George Liska, *Nations in Alliance* (Baltimore: Johns Hopkins Press, 1962.)

[6] Bruce Russett, *Community and Contention* (Cambridge: MIT Press, 1963).

[7] Richard Rosecrance and Raymond Dawson, 'Theory and Reality in the Anglo-American Alliance', *World Politics*, vol. 19 (October 1966).

[8] See, for example, Miriam Camps, *Britain and the European Community* (London: Oxford University Press, 1964); Uwe Kitzinger, *The Challenge of the Common Market* (Oxford: Basil Blackwell, 1962); also, Kitzinger, *Diplomacy and Persuasion* (London: Thames and Hudson, 1973).

[9] Examples for the period before British membership of the Community include John Pinder, *Europe Against de Gaulle* (London: Pall Mall Press, 1963); Hans Joachim Heiser, *British Policy with Regard to Unification Efforts on the Continent* (Leyden: Sythoff, for the Council of Europe, 1959). Since 1973, a number of articles in the *Journal of Common Market Studies* have also examined this aspect.

[10] See Drew Middleton, *The Supreme Choice* (London: Secker and Warburg, 1963); Lionel Gelber, *The Alliance of Necessity* (New York: Stein and Day, 1966). For a more detailed comparison, see David Calleo, *Britain's Future* (London: Hodder and Stoughton, 1968).

[11] Karl Kaiser, 'The Interaction of Regional Subsystems', *World Politics*, vol. 21 (October 1968), p. 86.

[12] Kaiser suggests that, in examining interaction, a distinction be made between 'overlapping' and 'non-overlapping' subsystems (ibid., p. 93).

[13] Liska has noted that 'Alignments are always instrumental in structuring the state system, sometimes in transforming it' (op. cit., p. 12).

[14] Karl Deutsch et al., *Political Community and the North Atlantic Area* (Princeton: Princeton University Press, 1957), p. 49.

[15] Joseph Nye, 'Comparative Regional Integration: Concept and Measurement', *International Organization*, vol. 22 (Autumn 1968), p. 858.

[16] See Joseph Nye, 'Patterns and Catalysts in Regional Integration', *International Organization*, vol. 19 (Autumn 1965), p. 871; and Ernst Haas and Phillippe Schmitter, 'Economics and Differential Patterns of Political Integration', in *International Political Communities: An Anthology* (Garden City: Anchor Books, 1966), p. 261.

[17] Nye, 'Comparative Regional Integration', p. 858.

[18] Ernst Haas, 'The Uniting of Europe and the Uniting of Latin America', *Journal of Common Market Studies*, vol. 4, no. 4 (June 1967), p. 328.

[19] Karl Kaiser, 'The US and EEC in the Atlantic System: The Problem of Theory', *Journal of Common Market Studies*, vol. 4, no. 4 (June 1967) p. 410.

[20] See the discussion of background conditions in Deutsch et al., op. cit., chapter 2, and Haas and Schmitter, op. cit., pp. 266–8.

[21] The concept of 'core power' is presented in Deutsch et al., op. cit., pp. 37–9; and Liska, op. cit., p. 87.

[22] William Riker, *The Theory of Political Coalitions* (New Haven: Yale University Press, 1962), p. 44.

[23] See Hans J. Morgenthau, *Politics Among Nations* (New York: Alfred Knopf, 1960), p. 183.

[24] In theory, each partner could gear its policies toward agreement with those of the other. Yet this would make maintenance of the alliance between them an end in itself. While such an analysis might be appropriate for a strict integration study, it presents a deviant case for interstate relations. See Ernst Haas, 'International Integration', in *International Political Communities*, on types of compromise in international relations.

[25] In the same vein, Stuart Scheingold uses the term 'policy arena', which 'implies a search for any indications of collectively distinctive foreign policy even if it is in the form of policy coordination rather than real joint policy-making.' Stuart Scheingold, 'The North Atlantic Area as a Policy Arena', *International Studies Quarterly*, vol. 15, no. 1 (March 1971), p. 51.

[26] See the discussion of this point in Ronald Inglehart, 'Trends and Non-trends in the Western Alliance', *Journal of Conflict Resolution*, vol. 12, no. 1 (March 1968), p. 122.

[27] Stanley Hoffmann's assessment is relevant here. 'The common values

and intense relations across borders which exist within the transnational society indicate what the attitudes and interests of the citizens are likely to be but do not determine either the policies of the governments or the nature of the political institutions and legal obligations that the governments may establish throughout the area.' Hoffmann, 'Discord in Community,' in Francis Wilcox and H. Field Haviland, Jr (eds), *The Atlantic Community: Progress and Prospects* (New York: Frederick Praeger, 1963), p. 11.

28 Nye, 'Patterns and Catalysts', p. 871.
29 'Europe' denotes the European Community and its member nations.
30 Kaiser, 'Interaction of Regional Subsystems', p. 105.
31 Nye, 'Patterns and Catalysts', p. 882.

PART I

ECONOMIC RELATIONS

2 Britain's Economy:
(1) History and Capabilities

There are strong arguments for beginning this study with economic relations. On the theoretical side, much of integration literature suggests that economic relations – non-controversial, less emotional, 'low' politics – are the necessary starting point for building a unification effort. It is from here that 'spillover' into other sectors, if it is to come, must begin.

In the second place, both the European Economic Community and the European Coal and Steel Community are, at least in a formal sense, economic institutions. Thus, as an international actor, the European Communities have had their most immediate impact on international economic relations.

There is, however, a third and even more compelling reason for focusing initially on this sector. The economic context is crucial in understanding Britain's postwar experience – indeed, it can be argued that Britain's political and military fortunes have been primarily a function of her economic condition.

Three historical factors need to be mentioned as a basis for understanding the postwar period. As a small island with a dense population, Britain has been unable for nearly a century to produce or grow all the goods she needed, and thus has had to rely very heavily on foreign commodities. The imperative to trade, and to trade well, is a basic fact of life which has had a profound influence on Britain's actions in the international sphere.

Trading well has meant being able to pay for the goods needed. This has been done in three ways. First, Britain has been, for the most part, an industrial and technological leader in the world. Thus, she has always had commodities which were in demand and for which she could obtain favourable prices.[1] Secondly, she has exerted a major effort in invisible exports, that is, the provision of services to persons living abroad. As an example, for many years London was known as the financial capital of the world, and the expertise of the City of London is still highly valued.[2] Finally, through a complex of international contacts and agreements, Britain has succeeded in obtaining many of the goods she has needed at relatively low prices. Butter and mutton from New Zealand are only the best-publicised examples.

The second consideration is the Commonwealth. In addition to its historical and psychological importance, this world-wide grouping has been of crucial economic significance to the British. Indeed, until 1967 the Commonwealth

15

was still the United Kingdom's single largest trading partner. Moreover, the use of sterling within the Commonwealth was a major factor in the development of the pound as an international currency.[3] Thus, there were material as well as sentimental factors which held the Commonwealth together. These had to be evaluated by the British as they contemplated the reordering of their international economic relations in the postwar period.

In the nineteenth century, Britain became a major world power, with considerable military might and global political influence. This status carried over into the twentieth century, even as its economic underpinnings came into question. Other nations with larger resource bases underwent their own industrial revolutions, thus reducing Britain's relative strength. Still, Britain's power was significant, as her effort in the Second World War demonstrated.

The result of the war constitutes a third important factor. It is a supreme historical irony that Britain's achievement in that struggle was both a prelude and a contributing factor to her subsequent economic decline. The connection is both direct and indirect. As one economist has noted, 'For Britain, military victory came close to being economic disaster.'[4] The war effort required an enormous expenditure of resources. Yet the economic pressure continued after 1945. The close of the war brought an abrupt termination of the American lend-lease programme at a time when British needs were, in fact, expanding. As the markets of the other nations of Europe were reopened after the war, countries which exported raw materials, Britain's chief import, also instituted more stringent payment requirements at a time when Britain's financial position was particularly weak. In the years following the war, Britain, whose industrial plant was not so heavily damaged by the war, did not participate in the widespread rebuilding of factories that occurred on the Continent and undoubtedly contributed to economic rebirth. And, finally, there was a psychological factor, namely the fact that the British had won the war and continued to think of themselves as a Great Power.[5] The habits which accompanied that attitude were hard to break. A feeling, held by some on the Continent, that a fundamental reordering was required, was not widespread in the United Kingdom. After all, Britain had been successful. Why change?[6]

In fact, the very factors which had been to Britain's advantage in the past no longer sufficed. Still an island which was not self-sufficient, still maintaining international ties and commitments, Britain's resources did not prove adequate to support her historical position.

Britain's changing capabilities

One statistic used to measure a nation's economic health is gross domestic product (GDP). While still one of the largest in the world, the British GDP has not kept pace with that of other major industrial nations. Some comparative figures for the North Atlantic area are shown in Table 2.1. They demonstrate that the United Kingdom has fallen behind both the United States and the rest of Western Europe. Moreover, they have had serious political implications. Certainly the figures helped to convince British leaders to seek membership in the EEC. An OECD study found that for the period 1958–67, the British GDP increased by 3·3 per cent, while the figure for the United States was 4·7 per cent, for France 5·8 per cent, and for West

Table 2.1

Gross Domestic Product:
Comparative statistics, 1958–1972

(1) GDP in million units of account (ua) at current prices
and current exchange rates

	UK	EEC	USA
1958	63·9	165·1	452·9
1959	67·4	169·0	489·1
1960	71·5	190·8	509·0
1961	76·3	212·6	525·7
1962	79·9	234·7	565·9
1963	84·9	258·1	596·3
1964	92·7	285·4	638·9
1965	99·5	309·6	692·1
1966	106·2	333·5	758·6
1967	109·9	353·0	803·6
1968	103·6	384·5	874·8
1969	110·6	428·6	942·6
1970	120·9	484·9	999·5
1971	134·6	535·7	1075·3
1972	147·9	602·1	1085·5

(2) GDP in million units of account (ua) at 1970 prices
and 1970 exchange rates

	UK	EEC (6)	EEC (9)	USA
1963	100·4	334·6	448·9	751·2
1964	106·0	354·2	475·2	791·5
1965	108·2	372·1	495·9	841·5
1966	110·3	385·9	512·3	897·3
1967	112·9	398·0	527·7	922·0
1968	116·8	421·4	555·8	968·0
1969	118·1	450·9	587·9	994·5
1970	120·6	477·2	617·2	983·2
1971	123·3	494·6	638·1	1014·3
1972	127·2	515·2	663·5	1076·2
1973	134·0	543·8	699·9	1136·9

Source: Statistical Office of the Community, *Eurostats*

Germany 4·8 per cent.[7] For the same period, British per capita GNP rose at an annual rate of 2·5 per cent, compared with a Community average increase of 4 per cent.[8]

If these figures helped to move the British toward Community membership, they also reflected a growing economic weakness which was highlighted, not overcome, by the initial period of participation in the EEC. The following tables showing annual percentage changes of GDP and, perhaps more dramatically, relative shares of the entire Community's GDP, suggest that Britain's bargaining for a political role has been from a position of increasing economic weakness.

A similar pattern is evident for industrial production. From 1950 to 1958, the British growth rate was noticeably less than that of the six nations which were to form the European Community. Moreover, comparisons for the period from 1958 to 1967 are even worse. For example, Belgium, the Community member with the lowest growth rate before 1958, showed a sharp improvement in industrial production after the creation of the Common Market, while Britain still continued to lag behind. The *relative* decline in Britain's industrial production is shown clearly by the post-1958 period, as both the EEC and the United States grew at faster rates.

These statistics clearly had an impact in Britain. In 1961, Harold Macmillan contended that entry into the Common Market would provide a 'brisk shower' of stimulation for British industry. Business leaders were in the forefront of the move towards a European link, and there was general optimism that Britain's industries could survive, and indeed in many cases thrive, in the competitive atmosphere of Europe. As Tables 2.1 to 2.4 indicate, the overall performance of British industry has been relatively sluggish. Still, there are some outstanding exceptions, such as Unilever, ICI, International Computers and British Petroleum.[9] These firms have demonstrated an ability to compete in the international market. Moreover, Britain's record in advanced technological fields has been the best in Western Europe.[10] Indeed, the British like to think that they hold the key to advanced industrial progress in Europe.[11]

Even the large firms have been having trouble, though. One dilemma faced by successive British governments is whether to provide public funds to assist potentially strong firms through difficult times. In particular, this was a problem for the Conservative government, which wanted firms to be able to compete in the European markets, but had philosophical reservations about public assistance. This ambivalence was demonstrated in the decisions to let Upper Clyde Shipbuilders go bankrupt, to delay before providing assistance to Rolls Royce, but to move quickly to the aid of International Computers.[12]

The Labour government does not have the same philosophical reservations, but their condition, i.e. public control to accompany public funds, was not

Table 2.2

European Community:
volume increase of GDP, 1966–74 (annual rates as percentage)

	1966–71	1972	1973	1974
Denmark	4·6	5·1	3·8	2·0
West Germany	4·4	3·0	5·3	1·9
France	5·8	5·5	6·0	5·2
Ireland	4·4	3·2	6·0	3·5
Italy	5·2	3·2	5·9	5·0
Netherlands	5·6	4·3	4·7	3·3
Belgium	4·7	5·2	5·7	4·0
Luxembourg	3·3	4·6	7·4	4·5
United Kingdom	2·2	2·3	5·6	−0·9
Community	4·4	3·7	5·6	2·7

Source: *Bulletin of the European Communities*, Supplement 7/74

Table 2.3

Member states' relative share in Community's GDP
calculated at current market exchange rates, 1972–74
(percentages)

	1972	1973	1974
Denmark	2·5	2·6	2·8
West Germany	31·0	33·0	33·6
France	23·2	23·9	23·2
Ireland	0·7	0·6	0·6
Italy	14·2	13·2	13·2
Netherlands	5·5	5·8	6·0
BLEU	4·4	4·5	4·7
United Kingdom	18·5	16·4	15·9
Community	100	100	100

The rates for 1972 and 1973 are the average rates for the year; those for 1974 are estimated on the basis of the monthly averages up to September.

Source: *Bulletin of the European Communities*, Supplement 7/74

Table 2.4a

Indices of industrial production (excluding building, food, beverages, tobacco)

1953 = 100

	Germany	France	Italy	Netherlands	Belgium	Luxembourg	The Six	UK	USA
1950	72	89	78	88	93	89	80	94	82
1951	85	99	89	91	106	99	92	98	89
1952	91	98	91	91	100	109	95	95	92
1953	100	100	100	100	100	100	100	100	100
1954	112	109	109	111	106	103	110	108	94
1955	129	117	119	119	116	116	122	114	106
1956	139	128	128	124	123	124	132	114	109
1957	147	139	138	127	124	126	140	116	110
1958	152	145	143	127	116	121	144	114	102

1958 = 100

	Germany	France	Italy	Netherlands	Belgium	Luxembourg	The Six	UK	USA
1958	100	100	100	100	100	100	100	100	100
1959	108	101	111	111	105	104	106	105	114
1960	122	111	129	124	113	114	119	113	117
1961	129	117	145	130	119	117	127	113	118
1962	134	123	159	137	127	112	135	114	128
1963	139	130	173	144	137	113	142	119	135
1964	152	140	175	158	147	124	152	128	144
1965	161	142	184	169	150	125	158	132	157
1966	163	151	207	181	153	120	167	133	172
1967	160	155	225	188	153	120	170	132	173

Sources: OEEC *General Statistical*; EEC *General Statistical Bulletin*

Table 2.4b

Indices of industrial production

1970 = 100			
	UK	EEC*	US
1968	96	87	99
1969	100	95	104
1970	100	100	100
1971	100	102	100
1972	102	108	108
1973	111	116	118

*Eight, excluding Denmark.
Source: OECD, *Main Economic Indicators*, 1974

greeted with enthusiasm.[13] Moreover, as one astute observer of the British scene has observed, this sort of intervention may well be counterproductive in the long run:

> I would guess that extensive new plant investment is unlikely to be lastingly profitable in Britain (in several major fields). . . . If Britain tries to prop up dying industries . . . we will find that our standard of living is having to fall to compete with Brazilian, Mexican and Taiwanese standards.[14]

There is, as of yet, no clear evidence that Common Market membership has provided the needed stimulus for British industry. The time has been brief and British industry has continued, for the most part, to support the Community and to be hopeful about the long term prospects.[15] In the meantime, however, British industrial strength has continued to decline.

One contributory factor which is cited by some commentators is the state of labour relations in the United Kingdom. Indeed, the British worker on strike has become almost a national stereotype. As the following figures demonstrate, the image has some validity, at least in comparison with other Western European nations. Table 2.5a indicates that by international standards Britain's labour problem may not be extraordinary. However, an examination of Table 2.5b shows that the comparisons within Western Europe are less encouraging. Moreover, the magnitude of the problem has been growing in recent years.

The issue is not a trivial one and its impact is not limited to damaged images. There is a certain irony, in fact, in de Gaulle's having cited labour disputes as one of the indicators of fundamental economic weakness which compelled him to veto Britain's EEC application in 1967.[16] Harold Wilson was able to respond that France's record was even worse, but, since then, the economic impact of strikes for Britain has increased.

In the first place, Britain's export capability is damaged to the extent that foreign buyers feel that production and delivery may be uncertain. In addition, lack of confidence in the labour situation has led to the withdrawal of some foreign investment in Britain. For example, the Ford Motor Company decided early in 1971 to build a major new plant in West Germany rather than

Table 2.5

Days lost through industrial disputes

a: Days lost per 1000 employed

	Averages for:		
	1963–67	1968–72	1963–72
Australia	378	900	639
Belgium	168	414	291
Canada	890	1724	1307
Denmark	104	68	86
Finland	414	916	665
France	364	277*	325*
Germany (GFR)	34	74	54
India	686	1264	975
Irish Republic	1208	964	1086
Italy	1050	1912	1481
Japan	200	226	213
Netherlands	16	56	36
New Zealand	184	354	269
Norway	74	18	46
Sweden	26	62	44
Switzerland	10	2	6
United Kingdom	184	968	576
United States	930	1534	1232

b: Days lost, thousands

	1970	1971	1972	1973
Belgium	1431·6	1240·9	353·8	866·0
Denmark	102·0	20·6	21·8	3901·2
France	1742·2	4528·8	3755·3	3914·6
Germany (GFR)	93·2	4483·7	66·0	563·1
Irish Republic	1007·7	273·8	207·0	206·7
Italy	18276·5	12948·8	17060·0	20402·3
Luxembourg	0	0	0	0
Netherlands	262·8	96·9	134·2	583·8
United Kingdom	10980·0	13551·0	23909·0	7197·0

Sources: a: British Information Service, 'Survey of Current Affairs', December 1973; b: European Community Information Office, *General Statistics of the Community*

in Britain precisely because of this problem. The impact is not easily transferable into quantitative terms but, by inference from the overall record of economic performance and through the statements of key officials, this factor would seem to be significant.

Indeed, the best indicator of awareness of the problem is the series of efforts by recent British governments to deal with labour relations. Apparently, the Labour government in the late 1960s seriously considered labour relations legislation, but ran out of time and public support.[17] One of the major priorities of Edward Heath's Conservative government after 1970 was the passage of the Industrial Relations Bill to put some legal structure around the operation of unions. The bill generated one of the longest debates in recent parliamentary history and was finally approved in 1971. The intent, clearly, was to give the government a mechanism for stabilising labour relations, with prospective membership in the European Community very much in mind, but the measure did not succeed either in terms of controlling strikes or in terms of Heath's political fortunes.

In the midst of growing economic problems (in particular a costly strike by coal miners), Heath called an election in February 1974 on the issue of obtaining a mandate to control the unions. He got neither a mandate nor a parliamentary majority. Moreover, one of the first steps of the new Labour government was to announce its intention to repeal the Industrial Relations Act, a measure that was accomplished by the summer.

Labour's new approach was the 'social contract', which amounted to voluntary wage restraint by the unions. The issue is still a very live one, although whether it is a fundamental *cause* of British economic decline does seem somewhat debatable. What is not disputed is that it is a contributory factor. An expanding prosperous economy, whether stimulated by Community membership, or North Sea oil, or something else, might well 'solve' over a period of time the problem of labour relations. With the economy going in the other direction, however, labour relations have worsened.

Changes in the cost of living represent a final indicator of economic health. At the same time as Britain has suffered a slow rate of economic growth, she has also experienced an above average level of inflation. Indeed, the term 'stagflation' was first coined in reference to the British economy.

As Table 2.6 shows, consumer price increases in Britain have been consistently among the highest in Western Europe. The increases for 1973 and 1974, the first two years of Common Market membership, were even higher than usual, and contributed to the political debate on the wisdom of being in the Community. Supporters of membership pointed to the unprecedentedly rapid rise in world commodity prices, particularly oil, and the devaluation of the pound as principal factors which would have affected Britain irrespective

Table 2.6

Changes in consumer prices, 1971–74

	1971	1972	1973	1974	Feb.	Mar.	Apr.	May	June	1974 July	Aug.	Sept.	Oct.	Nov.	Dec.
								Percentage of annual increase							
World	6·0	5·8	9·6	15·0	13·9	14·2	14·5	14·7	15·0	15·5	15·4	15·9	16·2	16·2	15·9
Developed Areas	5·3	4·8	7·8	12·9	11·8	11·9	12·3	12·4	12·7	13·3	13·0	13·6	14·1	14·2	13·9
Industrial Countries	5·1	4·5	7·6	12·6	11·6	11·7	11·9	12·1	12·4	13·0	12·8	13·4	13·9	14·0	13·6
United States	4·3	3·3	6·2	11·0	10·0	10·2	10·1	10·6	11·0	11·6	10·9	11·9	12·0	12·2	12·2
Canada	2·9	4·8	7·6	10·9	9·6	10·4	9·9	10·9	11·4	11·3	10·8	10·8	11·6	11·9	12·4
Japan	6·3	4·8	11·8	22·7	23·6	21·7	23·3	21·3	21·7	23·0	22·8	21·9	25·5	24·6	21·5
Industrial Europe	6·2	6·1	8·1	12·2	10·6	11·0	11·5	11·8	11·9	12·5	12·8	13·3	13·7	13·8	15·6
Austria	4·7	6·3	7·5	9·5	8·5	8·9	9·8	9·6	10·2	10·0	9·9	10·1	10·0	9·5	9·7
Belgium	4·3	5·5	7·0	12·6	8·3	9·4	10·3	11·6	12·6	13·7	14·5	15·7	15·9	16·3	15·7
Denmark	5·8	6·6	9·3	15·3	13·6	13·8	14·2	14·3	15·3	15·9	16·0	16·6	16·8	16·6	15·5
France	5·5	5·9	7·3	13·6	11·5	12·2	13·2	13·5	13·9	14·4	14·5	14·7	14·9	14·9	15·2
Germany	5·3	5·5	6·9	7·0	7·6	7·2	7·1	7·2	6·9	6·9	7·0	7·3	7·1	6·5	5·9
Italy	4·8	5·7	10·8	19·1	14·2	16·0	16·3	16·2	16·8	18·4	20·3	23·0	24·3	25·2	24·5
Netherlands	7·5	7·8	8·0	9·6	8·8	9·2	8·8	8·7	8·9	9·5	9·7	10·4	10·7	11·0	10·9
Norway	6·2	7·3	7·5	9·5	8·9	9·0	8·8	8·7	8·2	8·8	10·0	10·3	10·2	10·5	11·3
Sweden	7·0	6·5	7·0	9·8	10·2	10·9	10·1	8·3	8·3	8·2	9·0	9·8	11·3	12·0	11·1
Switzerland	6·6	6·7	8·7	9·8	10·0	9·6	8·8	9·9	9·6	9·8	10·5	11·3	9·8	9·0	7·5
United Kingdom	9·4	7·1	9·1	15·9	13·1	13·5	15·2	16·0	16·5	17·1	16·8	16·0	17·1	18·3	19·2

Source: International Monetary Fund, *International Financial Statistics*, vol. 28, no. 5 (May 1975).

of membership.[18] High wage settlements have also contributed to the problem. Whatever the cause, however, the economic effect has been serious.

At one level, the total economic picture provoked a re-evaluation of the economic costs of Community membership and of the need for various adjustment mechanisms within the EEC. The continuing deterioration also raises the question of whether Britain can exert real influence in the world in economic, military, or political terms; that is, whether she can play a role is highly dependent on what she can bring to that role. Certainly the economic picture has been a dreary one.

These indicators are measures of the relative growth and dynamism of the British economy as well as of its stability. They reveal that, in comparison with other industrial nations, Britain has been falling behind. The figures do not mean that Britain has collapsed economically, but while growth need not be a goal in and of itself, it does have a bearing both on the domestic standard of living and on the competitive ability of the United Kingdom in the international economic sphere. The crucial issue has been that of making choices. First, what level of affluence is Britain able to afford? Secondly, what sort of international position can she afford? Thirdly, what balance is to be maintained between her international and her domestic economic concerns?

Notes

[1] See the discussion of the relationship between trade and technology on pages 72–4.

[2] The importance of invisible trade has increased as the balance of trade in manufactured goods has deteriorated.

[3] Roy Harrod, *The British Economy* (New York: McGraw-Hill, 1963), p. 117.

[4] J. M. Livingstone, *Britain and the World Economy* (Baltimore: Penguin Books, 1966), p. 45.

[5] See the discussion of this point in Richard Mayne, *The Community of Europe* (New York: W. W. Norton, 1962), p. 136.

[6] In some senses, of course, the early postwar period under a Labour government was a time of change and adjustment. Yet a fundamental restructuring of the British economy was not accomplished, nor was the claim to world power status relinquished. For one discussion of this period, see Arthur Marwick, *Britain in the Century of Total War* (Boston: Little, Brown, 1968).

[7] OECD, *Economic Outlook* (July 1970).

[8] HMSO, *Britain and the European Communities: An Economic Assessment* (Cmnd. 4289, February 1970), para. 63.

[9] Another British firm which might be included in this list is Rolls Royce. The financial difficulties which developed in early 1971 are somewhat ironical. The winning of the contract for the RB-211 engine for Lockheed's Tri-Star aircraft was considered a major achievement and evidence of British technological advancement. The subsequent difficulties were mainly the product of over-extension and financial miscalculation rather than technological deficiency on the part of Rolls Royce. For many, this incident reinforced the conclusion that Britain needed a larger base, of both resource input and market size.

[10] This was acknowledged by the Commission of the European Community in its appraisal of Britain's 1967 application. See *Opinion of the Commission of the European Communities on the Applications for Membership Received from the United Kingdom, Ireland, Denmark and Norway* (Brussels, 29 September 1967), para. 147. In basic research, the Commission referred specifically to theoretical, nuclear, and solid state physics, chemistry and biology. The technological fields mentioned were aeronautics and engines, electronics and computers, atomic energy and chemistry.

[11] See, for example, the remarks of Fred Catherwood, Director General of Britain's National Economic Development Office (*The Times*, 8 September 1970).

[12] *The New York Times* (9 August 1971).

[13] For example, the Hawker Siddeley Company apparently abandoned the HS-146 project in 1974 rather than accept government control.

[14] Norman Macrae, 'The People We Have Become', *The Economist*, special supplement (28 April 1973), p. 25.

[15] The Confederation of British Industry did a study among its members in early 1974 and urged the Labour government to stay in the Common Market. See 'The CBI Backs Europe', *European Community* (May 1974). The business sector gave strong support to a 'yes' vote in the referendum.

[16] Press conference (27 November 1967).

[17] Harold Wilson's account acknowledges that legislation was considered, but suggests that a choice was made against it. See *The Labour Government 1964–1970: A Personal Record* (London: Weidenfeld and Nicolson, 1971), pp. 641–64. For another view, see Peter Jenkins, *The Battle of Downing Street* (London: Charles Knight, 1790).

[18] See for example, 'British Food Prices and the Common Agricultural Policy', *Background Note*, Commission of the European Communities (27 September 1973).

3 Britain's Economy: (2) Integration and Adjustment

At this point, a brief review of the theory of economic integration is needed. Bela Balassa has offered the following definition of economic integration: the 'abolition of discrimination between economic units belonging to different national states.'[1] Indeed, this is the most typical way of thinking about regional economic groupings. However, a useful addition, made by John Pinder, is more mindful of political implications. In it he distinguishes between negative and positive economic integration: regarding the former, he concurs with Balassa and others; positive economic integration, on the other hand, is defined as 'the formation and application of coordinated and common policies in order to fulfill economic and welfare objectives other than the removal of discrimination.'[2] This is the same line of thought adopted by the founders of the European Communities as well as by functionalist theorists of integration.

It is only from this dual approach that the full impact of the Common Market on Britain can be seen. In the first place, the British have had a negative concern: the fear of being shut out, out of traditional trading markets and out of a growing, prosperous community.[3] The constant series of Anglo-European discussions, starting in 1956 when it first appeared clear to the British that a European Economic Community would actually come into existence, and continuing until the British decision in late 1960 or early 1961 to apply for membership of the Common Market, was motivated by this problem. Although several factors were involved, the role of the economic challenge in Macmillan's decision should not be underestimated.[4] In 1961, it was possible to argue for the short run economic benefits of EEC membership for Britain.

In later years, as Community policy became more firmly established, this argument had to be dropped. By the second application, it could be clearly seen that Britain would suffer short term economic losses if she joined the Community, although the exact cost of these was in dispute. This debate continued during the third, and finally successful, application. A 1970 White Paper estimated that overall balance of payments costs would fall between £100 million and £1,100 million, obviously too wide a range to afford any basis for judgment.[5] The assessment of the short term economic costs, and of

27

Britain's ability to bear them, continued even after membership was achieved and formed the basis for the Labour government's announcement in 1974 that it would seek a readjustment of the price paid for entry, that is, a reduction of the short term costs.[6] At the same time, even the Labour government seemed to accept the view that there could be long term economic gains from Community membership.

A discussion of long term economic benefits is implicitly a political determination and shifts to a more positive assessment of Britain's relationship with Europe. This area of positive economic integration has held the real attraction for the British in recent years. Indeed, this transformation in British thought is more in line with much of the thinking of the founders of the European Community, who never visualised the organisation as merely a customs union.[7] Discussions on economic and monetary union, regional policy, and social policy, among others, all demonstrate the intent to collaborate on a wide range of issues.

The positive attraction of EEC membership has been both general and specific. The prospect of membership in an expanding prosperous group led British industry and the preponderance of elite opinion in the United Kingdom to favour entry.[8] As a significant example, European projects in the advanced technological sector were apparently a critical determinant in Harold Wilson's decision to apply in 1967.[9] Similarly it was argued that a European monetary system would enable the British 'to unload the millstone of the sterling system while maintaining their ties with a world currency.'[10] Despite persistent dissenters and a worsening of Britain's economic position since joining in 1973, one of the continuing arguments for participation in the European Communities has been the long term dynamic potential of economic integration.[11]

The domestic policy implications of European Community membership for the British have had a direct impact on Britain's needs and on her ability to satisfy them. In this sense, assessments of the 'importance' of the European alignment are based on potential as well as on existing factors.

In the first place, far-reaching changes have had to be made in the internal functioning of the British economy. The best-known area, which was considered one of the keys to Britain's negotiations for membership, is the agricultural sector.[12]

Britain's policy, since the repeal of the Corn Laws in 1846, has been to subsidise her farmers directly from government funds while importing the great bulk of British food needs cheaply from abroad. In the European Communities, on the other hand, the agricultural sector has been protected by high import duties with farmers guaranteed a fixed price for their goods. These two different approaches reflect differing historical perspectives. For the British, agricultural imports from other Commonwealth nations represented both a source of relatively cheap food and an important link of economic interdependence. On the Continent, in contrast, the relevant historical considerations have been a desire to develop agricultural self-sufficiency and, not incidentally, a vocal and politically active agricultural class.

For the British, the Common Agricultural Policy involved a second kind of adjustment as well. The EEC system calls for the creation of a European Agricultural Guidance and Guarantee Fund. Contributions to the Fund come from the member states and are at present charged partially on a fixed formula and partially in relation to the level of agricultural imports of each member. The fund is used to meet the cost of price subsidies as well as to finance structural reforms of the European agricultural sector.

The disadvantages to the British of this system are clear. As a large food importer, Britain faces the prospect of being a major contributor to the Fund. Or, as anti-Common Market forces put it, the British have to pay more for their food and also have to pay the European Community to be allowed to do so.

While there were indications even before British entry that the Europeans recognised some deficiencies in the Common Agricultural Policy and that changes might be in the offing,[13] those changes were not going to take the form of adoption of the British agricultural system. After years of both formal and informal discussions of this topic, it was clear that the Community was not going to change the policy *in order* to make entry easier for Britain. Thus, when the British government voluntarily agreed in the autumn of 1970 to transform its agricultural system into one basically similar to that of the Community, this was widely seen as a major step toward Europe.[14] The British undoubtedly felt they could negotiate revisions after they got in, but they finally recognised the futility of trying to do so before, and thus a crucial adjustment was made. Even with that step, however, the details of the negotiations were difficult to conclude and left many in Britain dissatisfied.[15]

What happened after entry seemed to confirm the most dire warnings of the anti-marketeers in Britain. Food prices shot up in Britain, as much as 20 per cent in the first year of EEC membership. This factor alone contributed substantially to the dissatisfaction with Community membership in Britain and to the success of the Labour Party in making renegotiation of the terms of entry a political rallying point. This reaction persisted despite defenders of the Common Market, who pointed out that world food prices were rising even faster than Community prices, that British prices would have increased even more outside the Community, and that, in fact, the CAP had resulted in relatively stable food prices for the Community as a whole.[16]

The Labour government made the review of agricultural policy one plank of its renegotiation demands[17] and there was some receptiveness to the issue, partly because the Germans also had some grievances about the CAP.[18] The Community agreed to an examination of the basic agricultural policies and, at the same time, made provision for occasional concessions to specific British needs in the agricultural sector.[19]

The dilemma of agriculture highlights the kinds of obstacles faced in achieving economic integration. One is time-span. While there *might* be long term adjustments of a beneficial nature in the CAP, the short term price increases have tended to obscure all else. Similarly, the impact of the CAP is calculated by each country by itself, almost as if agricultural policy was the only aspect of Community membership. Yet, clearly, there are a number of other areas of policy adjustment whose impact may be far different from that of the CAP.

One such area is regional policy. There are economically depressed areas in the United Kingdom whose plight will worsen in the larger Europe.[20] Still, in the Commission's not overly-optimistic appraisal of the British application of 1967, this difficulty was not seen as damaging to the whole European effort:

> If the Community were enlarged, it might be feared that the difficulties of the peripheral regions would increase, especially in Great Britain. It does not, however, seem that in an enlarged community the problem would be any other than in the Community of the Six.[21]

Those observations implied that the Community was adequately dealing with the problem of the underdeveloped areas of the original six members. In fact, however, the first general proposal to develop a Community regional policy was not made until October 1969. Since then, numerous approaches and plans have been discussed and some progress toward agreement has been made, with British membership and demands acting somewhat as a catalyst for the process.[22]

Three different kinds of questions have been raised about the issue of regional policy, although, ultimately they are closely related. The first is: what should be the goals of a regional policy? The limited, pragmatic answer has been to provide support and assistance to areas of high unemployment and low economic prosperity. This represents a reactive policy, one which essentially sets up a system of welfare transferral. In fact, the European Coal and Steel Community has been providing assistance – training programmes, housing subsidies, and displacement benefits – since 1954. In a sense, this approach treats the symptoms rather than the causes of economic depression.

Another answer to the question of goals is to encourage optimal development patterns and the efficient use of Community resources. To put it in different terms, this approach relates to the balancing of various economic sectors. Structural reform of different segments of the economy, investment incentives, and economic planning are all ingredients of this view. While the theoretical benefits of preventive actions are indisputable, the extent of cooperation needed involves a major test of political will. Thus it is not surprising that there has been hesitation and uncertainty in devising this kind of regional policy.

A second way of discussing regional policy is to focus on the kinds of regions to be given priority. The possibilities have included farming regions, depressed industrial areas, frontier regions, and peripheral regions. Up to now, the greatest headway has been made in farming areas, partly through the CAP's Guidance Fund and partly through the Community decision to begin a regional policy programme in the depressed agricultural areas.[23] That different members of the Community have differing regional needs underscores the sensitivity of the above priorities.

Similarly, there are differences over how to define a depressed area. Criteria which have been discussed have included unemployment rate, per capita income, and migration levels.[24] The obvious point is that different areas have differing kinds of economic problems, but all share a common desire for assistance. Moreover, the issue of a regional policy has been advanced as one adjustment mechanism within the context of economic and monetary union. The major obstacle, in fact, has been the tendency for each nation to calculate separately the costs and benefits of each programme and to evaluate them on that basis.

Thus, the third kind of question is how large the regional fund should be? In theoretical terms, the answer should relate to all of the previous considerations as well as to the levels and kinds of state aid which are already given. In fact, the figures discussed seem to be largely the product of political bargaining. In this vein, an agreement was announced at a summit meeting of the Nine in Paris in December 1974 to set up for a three-year period a regional fund of $1·6 billion,[25] 28 per cent of which was to be allocated to Britain.

In the aftermath of the summit, however, it became increasingly clear that previous sets of questions had not really been resolved. Moreover, the task undertaken by the British of evaluating the impact and costs of Common Market membership remained difficult. A commitment to a regional policy, adequately financed, with a significant share for the United Kingdom, has been a matter of high British priority. Working out the detailed functioning and measuring the impact of this is likely to take many years and will, at least in part, be determined by British political decisions.

A third adjustment mechanism, to be discussed in greater detail in the context of policy interaction, is monetary union. Two generalisations can be made here. First, in theory, these different policies are all related and should, logically, be evaluated as a package. As a practical political matter, however, there has been a tendency to treat them separately. The compelling logic of economic integration has not turned out to be so compelling.

Secondly, whether and how any of these policies work is directly tied to the extent of political commitment to them exhibited by the various members. Although, as this section indicates, the British have been undergoing adjustments in economic policy, those policies have, for the most part, been accepted reluctantly and with reservations. It cannot be proved that a whole-hearted political commitment would make these policies beneficial economically, but the lack of such a commitment has undoubtedly contributed to British difficulties. In this sense, the extent of adjustment of the British economy to the European Community has remained tentative and limited.

Summary

The last two chapters have highlighted Britain's main economic concerns. Her economic strength has diminished. The repercussions in the military and political sectors will be examined in later chapters. Meanwhile, the long term nature of economic decline has led, on the one hand, to a close scrutiny of present international economic arrangements and, on the other, to a continuing examination of alternatives.

In this context, Britain's relations with the United States and with the European Community can be considered. The main transactions are readily identifiable and are, in addition, easily quantifiable. First, trade is significant in both a theoretical and a historical sense. Theorists representing a variety of approaches to coalition behaviour have agreed that trade is a major component of economic ties.[26] In this sense, trade provides one potential link of interdependence in the international system.[27] As a second theoretical point, the economic benefits of trade, seen as one aspect of 'expectation of gain',[28] may provide a motivation for seeking closer relations in the economic sector. In addition, from a historical viewpoint, an examination of British economic capability makes it clear that trade is a crucial activity for meeting British needs, both in a commodity and in a financial sense. Absolute levels, relative levels, and patterns of change in trade flow all help to determine the 'importance' of these two subsystems for Britain.

Secondly, there is international investment. In the first place, foreign investment is related to trade. On the one hand, 'foreign investment will often be necessary to exploit the potential benefits offered by the widening of national markets through freer trade.'[29] In a general sense this may be the result of the 'lessening of uncertainty associated with national frontiers.'[30] On the other hand, foreign investment may be used as a mechanism for circumventing trade barriers.[31] A second theoretical significance of foreign investment transactions is as a measure of interdependence or perceived interdependence among nations.[32] Finally, the British government has been concerned with international investment because of the financial implications for Britain's balance of payments position. For these reasons, direct foreign investment can be seen as a component of the economic 'importance' to the British of different international alignments.

Regarding policy areas, these are drawn from the evaluation of Britain's economic condition. First, views on the nature of international trade agreements are vital to the United Kingdom. Policy interaction may not always coincide with the actual trade patterns within either subsystem. Distinctions and modifications are observable in the period being considered.

A second area is international monetary arrangements. The international role of sterling, balance of payments deficits, and speculative pressure on the pound have made this a significant issue for the British. Dissatisfaction with the international monetary system has been expressed in many different quarters, but not always for the same reasons.

These policy areas relate to the effort by the British to resolve their long term economic dilemma. They have been faced with the problem of trying to find answers to the three questions posed at the end of Chapter 2[33] in the face of a significant decline in economic strength. Harold Wilson, after his re-election in October 1974, commented that the British were facing the most formidable peacetime challenge of their lives.[34] His statement is hard to dispute.

Notes

[1] Balassa, *The Theory of Economic Integration* (Homewood, Illinois: Richard Irwin, 1961), p. 1.

[2] John Pinder, 'Positive Integration and Negative Integration', *The World Today*, vol. 24, no. 3 (March 1968), p. 90. See also Jan Tinbergen, *International Economic Integration* (Amsterdam: Elsevier, 1954), p. 76.

[3] De Gaulle reported that Harold Macmillan had expressed fears of a European trade war in June 1958 (*The Times*, 8 October 1970).

[4] For the argument that the application decision was made primarily on economic grounds see Kenneth Younger, *Changing Perspectives in British*

Foreign Policy (London: Oxford University Press for the Royal Institute of International Affairs, 1964), p. 11.

[5] HMSO, *Britain and the European Communities: An Economic Assessment.* Cmnd. 4289. See Norman Macrae, 'The Phoenix is Shortsighted,' special supplement to the *Economist*, 16 May 1970, for a more favourable economic assessment. The figures in the upper part of the range were, of course, seized upon by opponents of Common Market membership in Britain.

[6] HMSO, *Renegotiation of the Terms of Entry into the European Economic Community* (Cmnd. 5593, April 1974).

[7] In this respect, use of the term 'Common Market' is somewhat misleading.

[8] See the discussion of this point in Robert Pfaltzgraff, *Britain Faces Europe* (Philadelphia: University of Pennsylvania Press, 1969), especially chapter 2.

[9] See Wilson's speech to the Consultative Assembly of the Council of Europe, 23 January 1967; his speech to the House of Commons, 2 May 1967; and his proposal for a European Technological Community (Guildhall Speech), 13 November 1967.

[10] Christopher Layton, 'The Prizes of Monetary Union in Europe', *The Times*, (18 August 1970).

[11] For example, a London Chamber of Commerce and Industry survey in mid-1974 found overwhelming support for continuing membership. The reason cited most often was the potential for economic and industrial growth. See *European Community* (October 1974).

[12] See, for example, HMSO, *The Common Agricultural Policy of the European Economic Community* (Cmnd. 3274, May 1967).

[13] For example, Dr Sisco Mansholt, then Commission member in charge of agriculture, recommended a rationalisation and modernisation of the European agricultural system. These changes, he hoped, would enable the Community to reduce its surpluses as well as the size of the agricultural budget (*The Times*, 27 June 1970). This provoked an angry response by European farmers with demonstrations in Brussels, in March 1971.

[14] *The Times* (28 October 1970). In fact, the Conservative Party had pledged this change in 1965: see Conservative and Unionist Central Office, *Putting Britain Right Ahead: A Statement of Conservative Aims* (London, 1965).

[15] See Uwe Kitzinger, *Diplomacy and Persuasion*.

[16] See, Commission of the European Communities, 'British Food Prices and the Common Agricultural Policy', *Background Note* (September 1973).

[17] HMSO, *Renegotiation of the Terms of Entry*, Cmnd. 5593. See also the remarks of Fred Peart, Minister of Agriculture, to the Council of Ministers, 18 June 1974.

[18] In October 1974, under pressure from both the Germans and the British,

an agreement was reached to conduct a complete review of the Common Agricultural Policy.

[19] The most significant was an agreement to subsidise sugar prices.

[20] Some opponents of British membership argued that the entire United Kingdom would become a depressed area.

[21] *Opinion*, para. 110.

[22] See European Parliament, *The Effects, in 1973, on the United Kingdom of Membership of the European Community* (July 1974), ch. 3, p. 9.

[23] *European Community* (September 1971), p. 23.

[24] *The Economist* (21 April 1973).

[25] *Washington Post* (11 December 1974). By March 1975, the figure had been raised to $1·8 billion (*Baltimore Sun*, 5 March 1975).

[26] See, for example, Karl Deutsch et al., op. cit., p. 49; George Liska, op. cit., p. 14.

[27] See Richard Cooper, *The Economics of Interdependence* (New York: McGraw-Hill for the Council on Foreign Relations, 1968), p. 10.

[28] Ernst Haas, *The Uniting of Europe* (Stanford: Stanford University Press, 1957), chapter 1.

[29] Balassa, *Trade Liberalization Among Industrial Countries* (New York: McGraw-Hill, 1967), p. 126. See also Maxwell Stamp Associates, *The Free Trade Area Option* (London: The Atlantic Trade Study, November 1967), p. 59.

[30] Bela Balassa, *The Theory of Economic Integration*, p. 179.

[31] M. M. Postan, *An Economic History of Western Europe 1945–1964* (London: Methuen and Co., Ltd, 1967), p. 113.

[32] Cooper, op. cit., p. 82. See also Ernst Haas's comments in 'The Study of Regional Integration: Reflections on the Joy and Anguish of Pretheorizing', *International Organization*, vol. 24, no. 4 (Autumn 1970), p. 614.

[33] See page 25.

[34] *Washington Post* (29 October 1974).

4 Economic Policy: (1) Britain and Europe

The challenge presented by the EEC was the dominant feature on Britain's international economic horizon during much of the period of this study. In the first place, the decline in British economic strength was underscored by the growth and prosperity of the six members of the original EEC. Comparative figures have already been shown in a previous chapter, but what was even more significant for some British leaders was the potential for continued development by the Six. Thus the British have been trying to come to terms with the economic impact of the European Community on their own future, first by opposing the Common Market and, eventually, by becoming a member. Even that last step has not resolved Britain's long term economic dilemma, but the process of 'coming to terms' has led to major examinations of British economic policy.

Trade policy

The external adjustments which Britain has had to make have included developing new trading patterns. Part of this subject has already been considered in the matter of cheap foodstuffs. In this section, the British position on international trade agreements is reviewed. A detailed statistical breakdown will also be presented in the examination of trade transaction.

Whereas in the past Britain had 'important' trading ties with the United States, and more particularly with the Commonwealth, these were necessarily downgraded after Britain joined the EEC. In the case of the Commonwealth, the shift would have been even more dramatic if it had occurred soon after the Second World War. However, from the early 1960s onwards, the proportion of British trade with the rest of the Commonwealth decreased. Not only were the formal trading preferences between Britain and the rest of the Commonwealth eliminated, but Britain, in fact, had to discriminate against those nations after 1972. In turn, a preferential barrier was established around trade with the other members of the European Community.

It is from this perspective that the imperatives of internal adjustment are seen more clearly. For Britain to make a success of the new markets available to her, she will need to have more competitive, dynamic industries. The potential provided by a market of 280 million people with high consumption demands is clear.

Similarly, Britain's consumer-oriented population now has greater access to the goods of Western Europe. This could be a mixed blessing as far as Britain's balance of payments is concerned, although eventually the impact will also depend on the other adjustment processes worked out, such as a European monetary union and a regional policy.

With this background, it is possible to assess British–EEC interaction in the policy area of international trade. In the first place, the British had to assess the ability of this alignment to respond to their economic needs. In addition, however, the views which the British had on international trade issues were sometimes taken as measures of Britain's 'European-ness'. Thus, not only the extent of policy agreement but also the willingness to modify divergent views have been significant in the British–European subsystem.

It may well be that the basis for policy differences between Britain and the Common Market on international trade up to 1972 was institutional, that is, the UK was outside the Community's tariff barrier. She was the victim, not the beneficiary of the preferential trade agreements of the Community. Thus, different perspectives led to differing analyses of economic interest.

In 1958, Britain saw her trading interests as global, yet felt she could not ignore the development of the EEC. The attempt to reconcile her disparate needs was the proposal for a Free Trade Area, which would have given Britain access to the industrial markets of Western Europe while leaving intact the system of Commonwealth preferences which was the source of her supply of inexpensive foodstuffs.

While the proposal was not without its attractions for the Community, particularly the West Germans, the French veto was accepted by her Common Market partners because of their overriding loyalty to the Treaty of Rome and their desire for more comprehensive economic cooperation.[1] The differences were not so much of trade philosophy as of assessments of the impact of a particular idea. The Six did not want their project for economic progress to be diluted. The British, rather than being opposed to trade preferences, just did not want to be restricted by particular ones. The result was a rejection of the British proposal. On very practical grounds, the trade policies of Britain and the European Community were in direct conflict.

The same kind of consideration dominated British–European interaction on this issue after 1958. Britain had pressing needs which she hoped to satisfy through advantageous trading arrangements. This led to two approaches with respect to relations with the Community. On the one hand, there were three attempts to join the Common Market. Although the British, in all three cases, asked for certain concessions, they accepted the idea of a preferential trading block. The talk about 'inward' or 'outward' looking did not mean much in this respect. However, by 1971 Britain still had not succeeded in negotiating membership of the EEC. Since their economic needs still had to be satisfied, the British also put pressure on the Common Market from the outside. The Trade Expansion Act proposed in 1962 by President Kennedy was seen originally as a starting point for an Atlantic partnership, including broadly liberalised trade. The American proposal was strongly supported by the UK. With de Gaulle's veto of Britain's application in 1963 however, the prospective trade negotiations became instead a means of lessening the impact of being outside the Common External Tariff of the Community. During the Kennedy Round, the British generally sided with the Americans in advocating ambitious and far-reaching trade liberalisation, a view which found them at odds with the Six.[2] This did not, however, prevent a new Labour effort to negotiate membership in 1967.

During the third membership negotiations in 1970–71, trade issues continued to receive considerable attention. Again, though, the differences did not seem to be so much over trade philosophy as over the practical impact of restructuring patterns of British trade. To be sure, the British argued for special arrangements for developing Commonwealth nations and negotiations with the non-applicant EFTA members, but the hard trade issues involved British needs. A report by the Commission of the European Communities clearly pinpointed the difficult areas:

The negotiations with the United Kingdom really got under way in September 1970. By the beginning of May 1971, after six ministerial meetings, most of the major issues had been disposed of, including the Commonwealth and free movement of industrial and agricultural products, the freeing of capital movements, sterling balances, applications for tariff quotas, and a variety of matters relating to the institutions, ECSC and Euratom, the Community's contractural obligations, and so on. The only points still outstanding were the so-called 'awkward' ones, New Zealand butter, Britain's contribution to the Community's own resources, Commonwealth sugar and the fisheries problem.[3]

Indeed, the view of British trade policy as a problem-solving device was reinforced after Community membership was achieved. While the renegotiation proposal focused on Britain's contribution to the Community budget, the question of trade policy toward Commonwealth nations was again raised, particularly regarding agricultural goods. Moreover, the British managed to win a major concession from the Community on sugar imports, namely an agreement to subsidise for the British the difference between the international market and the Community price of sugar in 1975. However, this may well have been a political effort to increase the attractiveness of the Community for the British, at a time of continuing domestic debate about the merits of membership.

In summary, the state of trade policy interaction between the British and the Community, rather than evolving in a particular pattern, has been largely determined by two factors. First, the existence of institutional barriers, with the British first outside and then later inside, has been a key aspect. The existence of very specific British needs, with alternative options for meeting those needs, has been a second factor, sometimes reinforcing the first, sometimes conflicting with it. While this policy area does not seem to pose a major obstacle to future Anglo-European relations, neither has it had a binding effect up to now.

International monetary policy

The history of interaction in the area of international monetary policy has been somewhat different. For much of the postwar period, Britain tended to support plans for greatly expanded liquidity, a stand which put her alongside the United States against strong European, and especially French, opposition.[4]

Reorganisation of the international monetary system has been widely discussed as the international supply of reserves has seemed inadequate for the increased volume of international transactions.[5] In considering specific proposals, European opposition in previous years centred on the role of the dollar. The French, in particular, accused the United States of expanding her economic influence by maintaining constant deficits in her international accounts. Thus plans for expanding international liquidity were restricted by the emphasis on controls to be included in them.

To a certain degree, the position of the pound was subsumed in these deliberations by other international issues. The British wanted expanded and more flexible liquidity. Both because there was no immediate prospect of terminating the international status of sterling and because the British were not clearly in favour of that anyway, the issue was of considerable economic 'importance'. In this area, however, the patterns of interest of Britain and of the European Community did not, for the most part, coincide.

The issue was complicated by the interest of the Six in monetary union. This involved, on the one hand, the theoretical question of international payments adjustments and, on the other, the specific problems caused by the unique position of the United Kingdom. In its 1967 appraisal of Britain's application, the Commission stressed the need for close coordination of policy between Britain and the Community:

> There is one field where this point is of exceptional importance – monetary matters. For this is where the process of adjustment required of the British economy would be most necessary and most difficult, and where the present members of the Community would be exposed to the greatest risks.[6]

Article 108 of the Treaty of Rome provides for mutual assistance in the financial field. There was some fear that the British would constitute a permanent drain on the Community's resources. Indeed, this provided the rationale for de Gaulle's insistence that the British stabilise their economy *before* they be allowed to join the EEC.[7]

The British had attempted to deal with this problem in May 1967 when they declared that they would not invoke Article 108 in support of sterling's international role.[8] However, the Commission found this statement inadequate, observing that Article 108 might have to be used to ensure that the Community as a whole was not damaged.[9] In any case, a disavowal of one provision tends to miss the point of membership in an economic union.

During the third British application, the question of the role of sterling after Britain entered was not raised until a rather late point, March 1971. Despite British protests that the subject could be better dealt with after they had joined, France insisted that the sterling balances be wound down and that, ultimately, sterling be eliminated as a reserve currency.[10] The solution was a compromise, a British statement of intent by the chief negotiator, Geoffrey Rippon:

> We are prepared to envisage an orderly and gradual run-down of official sterling balances after our accession. We shall be ready to discuss after our entry into the Communities what measures might be appropriate to achieve a progressive alignment of the external chacteristics of and practices in relation to sterling with those of other currencies in the Community in the context of progress toward economic and monetary union in the enlarged Community. . . .[11]

In fact, some British have seen major opportunities in this area within the Community. Britain's ability to sustain an international currency has become increasingly doubtful. For example, the British decision to float the pound on 23 June 1972 was allegedly in response to speculative pressure rather than specific economic difficulties.[12] The British government looked towards the possibility of a joint European reserve fund to remedy this problem and made some very far-reaching proposals in March 1973.[13] While the British plan was not accepted, a more modest-sized pool was nevertheless instituted.

Curiously, that British position implied serious support for economic and monetary union even as progress toward it slowed to a crawl. The Werner Report, which was accepted by the Council of Ministers on 22 March 1971, committed the Community to move in stages toward full economic and monetary union by 1980. Since then, however, there have been a number of setbacks, including the British float, and the explicit commitment seems to have been set aside.

Yet, just as the British proposal for a reserve pool was motivated by very practical calculations, so economic conditions, international and intra-Community, may provoke renewed interest. Certainly the world monetary system has been disrupted in recent years by a number of developments. The changing role of the dollar and of American policy has been one factor. The economic policy announced by President Nixon in August 1971 may have marked the end of the old system, but the construction of a new one has not yet been accomplished. The 1973–74 oil crisis, which sharply redistributed world reserves, also underscored the need for new world monetary arrangements. Immediate attention was devoted to the need to 'recycle' oil profits, with competing American and European plans as well as unilateral steps by many industrial nations. These short-range activities have not yet led to a restructured international monetary system, however.

The international impact of any regional arrangement, such as a European monetary union, is debatable.[14] Whether the European effort goes forward, however, depends more on political and economic relations within the Community than on arguments about the international system. And, for just that reason, the British *may* end up being leading advocates of monetary union despite the supranational implications thereof. The prospects for monetary union have to be seen within the context of a whole series of adjustment mechanisms, or, more practically, trade-offs among the different members of the Community.

It has been generally observed that monetary union would mostly benefit Germany, which has the strongest economy, since the other Community members would no longer be able to increase their competitiveness through devaluation. Yet it is also clear that a compensating mechanism would also have to be provided for other nations, in order to prevent an unbalanced economic structure in Europe. Indeed, the movement towards a regional policy was explicitly tied to the impact of monetary union. The British have regarded a regional policy as critical to their own development in Europe, in the short term to lessen the budgetary impact of membership and in the long term to assist in a revitalisation of British industry. French policy has been to oppose monetary union, but the political dynamics, including re-evaluation of the Common Agricultural Policy, may lead to bargaining and significant concessions.

In a sense, the argument being presented here is that there may be merit in the neo-functionalist approach. Certainly the *possibility* of spillover and expansion is seen most clearly in this area. Political resistance has limited progress in the past and may continue to do so. *If* Europe is to move toward positive integration – a big if at a time when disintegration seems a possibility – then economic and monetary union would seem a prime candidate as the needed catalyst.[15]

In both of these policy areas, the initial pattern was one of divergent views. The ability of the alignment to satisfy British economic needs was limited prior to EEC membership. Community policy certainly did not move in the direction of the British position before then. In this sense, neither material gain nor increasing interdependence proved a building-block for British–EEC economic integration.

A second pattern, after de Gaulle's 1967 veto, was an increased willingness by the British to 'politicise' these economic issues,[16] that is, they developed their own policy positions in order to increase the prospects for overall agreement between Britain and the EEC. While there was neither joint policy-making nor detailed policy coordination within the subsystem, the latter development indicated a significant departure from the previous pattern. Such shifts reflected a British consciousness of 'expectation of gain' from economic relations in this alignment. In this sense, emphasis was on the potential rather than the actual 'importance' of the subsystem.

Since becoming a member of the Community, Britain has continued to focus on needs and benefits, but the pursuit of those may have positive implications for Community development. If the British can resolve their political uncertainty about membership, their economic needs are sufficiently great for them to perhaps have to support substantial progress in European economic integration. By then, however, the key question may be whether their views on economic policy carry significant political weight.

Notes

[1] Miriam Camps, *Britain and the European Community*, p. 172.

[2] For a discussion of this see Miriam Camps, *European Unification in the Sixties* (New York: McGraw-Hill for the Council on Foreign Relations, 1966), p. 130.

[3] Commission of the European Communities, *The Enlarged Community:*

Outcome of the Negotiations with the Applicant States (Brussels, 22 January 1972), p. 47.

4 See Calleo, op. cit., p. 82.

5 See Robert Triffin, *Gold and the Dollar Crisis* (New Haven: Yale University Press, 1961); Seymour Harris (ed.), *The Dollar in Crisis* (New York: Harcourt, Brace, 1961).

6 *Opinion*, op. cit., para. 97.

7 Press conference (27 November 1967).

8 James Callaghan in the House of Commons (10 May 1967).

9 *Opinion*, op. cit., para. 98.

10 *Washington Post* (18 April 1971).

11 HMSO, *The United Kingdom and the European Communities* (Cmnd. 4715, July 1971), para. 125.

12 Anthony Barber, Chancellor of the Exchequer, presented this view (*Hansard*, House of Commons, 29 June 1972, cols. 1700–14).

13 See the discussion by David Fouquet, 'Money Unstuck', *European Community* (May 1973), p. 7.

14 For a thoughtful discussion of this and related issues see Fred Hirsch, 'The Politics of World Money', *The Economist* (5 August 1972), pp. 55–68.

15 The Labour government in its White Paper recommending continued membership of the European Community, repeated its opposition to the existing plans for economic and monetary union (HMSO, *Membership of the European Communities: Report on Renegotiation*, Cmnd. 6003, March 1975, para. 46). However, the White Paper also noted 'the importance and value of consultation and cooperation with other member states on economic and monetary questions' (para. 51).

16 See Haas and Schmitter, op. cit., p. 262.

5   Economic Policy:
(2) Britain and the United States

No interest has been expressed in 'positive economic integration'[1] in the Anglo-American international subsystem. Given this, the matter of domestic policy adjustment is here a much less important consideration than it is for the British–European subsystem. In evaluating the 'importance' of this alignment, the emphasis has been on actual benefits, on satisfying British economic needs. In fact, agreement on international economic policy was a key aspect of Britain's relationship with the United States in the early postwar era. The starting point for that convergence was the shared interest in a system of stable international payments which goes back to the Atlantic Charter of 1941 and the Bretton Woods Agreement of 1944.[2] A second trend was agreement in principle on the benefits of trade liberalisation. From these common objectives, as well as from the overall closeness of Anglo-American relations, came interaction on a wide range of economic matters.

Trade policy

In the area of international trade, despite agreement on the principle of trade liberalisation, Anglo–American economic relations have not always been smooth or harmonious.[3] In the late 1950s, there was a fundamental clash of attitudes toward European economic integration. United States disapproval of the Free Trade Area proposal and her concurrent support of the Common Market strained the relationship with Britain. While British policy at this time was concerned with maintaining an optimal trade position for the United Kingdom, the United States saw that policy as damaging to American economic interests. Moreover, the two nations drew differing conclusions about the political ramifications of European economic integration. This basic disagreement was continued during the 1960 reorganisation of the OEEC into the OECD, with Britain in opposition to both the United States and the EEC.[4] This source of tension was finally relieved by the British decision to apply for membership of the European Community in 1961.

That decision led to a period of improved trade policy relations in the Anglo-American subsystem. The British application was one motivating factor in the Kennedy Administration's 'Grand Design'.[5] The specific vehicle was to be the Trade Expansion Act of 1962,[6] a request for broad trade negotiating powers which was seen as the foundation for a new Atlantic partnership. American officials took it for granted that Britain would soon be a member of the Common Market. In addition, one of the bill's provisions specifically applied to a European Community which included Britain.[7]

For their part, the British were quite receptive to the idea of an Atlantic partnership.[8] In the economic sector, the plan raised the prospect of greatly expanded trading markets for Britain. In addition, the United Kingdom would be able to maintain close economic relations with the United States even after joining the Common Market. Indeed, the possibility of improved relations was seen.

However, de Gaulle's veto of Common Market membership for Britain in January 1963 ended any such idea. Indeed, after the veto American policy-makers rejected the notion of a special commercial arrangement with Britain.[9] The Kennedy Round under GATT, which followed the Trade Expansion Act, saw Britain and the United States agreeing on the need for extensive tariff reductions. While improvements in the international trade situation resulted from the Kennedy Round, it was not as comprehensive as had been hoped originally and did not lead to closer cooperation in other sectors. These developments raised doubts about the ability of this subsystem to respond to Britain's long term economic needs.

The question of potential 'importance' was raised again during the second British attempt to join the Common Market in 1967. The idea of a North Atlantic Free Trade Area (NAFTA) attracted attention, albeit not official support, in Britain. Although the emphasis of the proposal was as an alternative if negotiations with the EEC failed, some of its supporters felt that NAFTA was preferable to British entry into the Community.[10] While there were variants, the basic idea was a free trade area which would include Britain, the United States, Canada, and some EFTA members. Moreover, this was to be exclusively a trade grouping with no interest in economic or political integration.

However, the plan has a fatal flaw: the United States showed almost no interest in it. Even though the proposal had been supported by some American legislators,[11] the idea was not taken very seriously by either the Johnson or the Nixon Administrations. Moreover, the British government continued to favour the Common Market option.[12] Thus, in a negative sense, the lack of enthusiasm for NAFTA by either member of the Anglo-American subsystem suggested a low potential for highly 'important' trade policy interaction.

The tendencies towards protectionism in the late 1960s in the United States Congress seemed to diminish further the prospects for NAFTA as well as to damage Anglo-American commercial relations in general. The Mills Trade Bill of 1970 threatened to reverse the trend toward freer trade and might have led to an Atlantic trade war if passed by Congress. In any such development, Britain would have been damaged and she went on record as being strongly opposed to the American trade legislation.[13]

Another indicator of a shift in American trade policy was reflected in the Nixon Administration's attitude toward the Common Market.[14] Domestic political and economic factors played a large role. Prominent among them were the shift in position of American trade unions in the face of a domestic economic slump, a continuing deficit in the US balance of trade, and President Nixon's promises to certain constituencies (particularly Southern textile manufacturers) during the 1968 campaign to protect them against foreign competition.[15] In this atmosphere, there was a growing awareness of and concern about the economic disadvantages to the United States of the European grouping. There were complaints that the Common Market was ignoring vital United States economic interests.[16] Thus US officials said that while the United States still favoured British entry into the EEC, she was less ready to pay an economic price for it than she had been in the past.[17]

American concern involved the general impact of expanding the Common Market as a trading block and the specific effect of certain key areas, particularly agriculture.[18] American misgivings about European policy in this sector had been evident for many years. The change in the British agricultural system, discussed previously, and Britain's subsequent entry into the Common Market, led to intensified US complaints.

From this point, Anglo-American trade relations have to be seen within the broader context of American–European trade relations. Indeed, the decreasing British leverage in Washington has been widely cited as one reason for Britain's joining the EEC. In this way, the possibility of affecting international trade issues may be re-established. The Labour government's White Paper urging continued Common Market membership was very explicit about this:

> The United Kingdom is more dependent on international trade than most countries, and the Government has been able to ensure that positions taken by the Community, which are of great importance for our trading and financial interests, reflect United Kingdom views.[19]

The pattern of future transatlantic trade relations is uncertain, but will undoubtedly be both economically and politically important. The United States and the European Community did succeed in negotiating an agreement under Article 24/6 of GATT to compensate the United States for the trade effects of British, Danish, and Irish entry into the Common Market,[20] but broader agreements may be more difficult to achieve.

In the first place, the ability to negotiate as a single unit has significant political implications for the Community, both internationally and internally.[21] Getting a broad negotiating mandate from the member states is at least as difficult for the Commission as it is for an American President to receive the kind of authority he wants from the United States Congress. From this perspective, the increased international weight which the British expect to carry will be dependent on separate national calculations of economic and political benefits and costs. That kind of issue has, in the past, yielded very slowly to far-reaching collaboration.

The second obstacle is the American view of world economic relations. Calleo and Rowland are not optimistic about the prospects for growing interdependence in the Atlantic Community, and suggest that United States policy, despite past rhetoric, is not likely to assist such a development.[22] Recent history – US trade legislation and the Nixon Administration's trade policy – would seem to support their argument. Such observations are less criticisms than reflections on the changed international situation.

A possible test of future relations is the re-named Tokyo Round of trade negotiations under GATT. Delayed for over five years, largely by American domestic political factors, these talks may reveal much about both the European and the American position in trade relations. The results, whether significant progress in eliminating trade barriers or an inability to reach any agreement of substance, will depend on political will, economic strength, and whether various views of international economic arrangements can be reconciled. It is a process that Britain, as an individual nation, can affect hardly at all. Her impact within a European block depends on the same set of factors mentioned above, which will be important internationally. Given that, her influence is far from certain, notwithstanding her stated interest.

International monetary policy

Britain and the United States were, as noted previously, at one time in general agreement on the need for increased international liquidity. These two nations were primarily responsible for the international monetary system which was established after the Second World War. In fact, the original British plan for postwar international monetary arrangements was more ambitious than the American version. The subject was not closed with the creation of the International Monetary Fund (IMF) in 1946. Rather, numerous proposals for an expansion of liquidity were considered in the following years. While not always agreeing on all details, Britain and the United States generally co-operated closely in these deliberations.

Anglo-American monetary interaction has not been limited to the institutional realm however. Table 5.1 shows the American postwar loan to Britain. The conditions attached to the postwar loan, particularly that of an early return to convertability of the pound, caused considerable dissension. Both the imbalance and the duality for Britain of the relationship are illustrated by this example. Then, as later, Britain saw no alternative but to take the assistance on American terms, and those terms were more mindful of American than British interests. Within that framework, US support for the pound in the following years continued to be vigorous, involving direct assistance in times of sterling crises, a demonstrated willingness to assist, which prevented greater pressure on the pound, and psychological backing

Table 5.1

Foreign loans secured by the United Kingdom, 1945–67

Loans	Date	Sterling* (£ million)
American line of credit	December 1945	931
Canadian line of credit	March 1946	297
South Africa	October 1947	80
Economic Cooperation Administration	October 1948	86
Belgium	September 1949	1
Portugal	September 1949	83
European Payments Union Loan	September 1950	218
liquidated in 1959 into a series of repayments to individual countries totalling £167 million:		
Austria	March 1959	3
Belgium	April 1959	24
Denmark	April 1959	less than 1
Greece	May 1959	less than 1
Germany	April 1959	96
Italy	April 1959	7
Netherlands	April 1959	21
Sweden	April 1959	9
Switzerland	May 1959	7
Mutual Security Aid	March 1952	17
Belgium	June 1952	9
Export–Import Bank	February 1957	89
Switzerland	October 1961	18
Export–Import Bank line of credit:	April 1966	19
military aircraft loans	January 1966	12
	August 1966	66
	July 1967	20
Swiss Bank Consortium	October 1967	37

*At rates applicable to date of loan
Source: *Hansard*, House of Commons (23 November 1967), cols. 415–16

for the role of sterling in the world economy. As Table 5.2 indicates, the United States has remained Britain's chief creditor.

With the dollar and the pound as the two world reserve currencies, the United States was especially sensitive to pressures on sterling as a possible prelude to dollar difficulties. This link and the significance of it were accepted as axiomatic for many years. In addition, Britain's financial problems tended to keep her economic relationship with the United States close because of the 'importance' of American help. However, this tie could only be maintained as

Table 5.2

International loans to the United Kingdom
outstanding at the end of the year, 1958–73 (£ million)

	Total outstanding	Total owed to US	Percentage of total owed to US
1958	2,127	1,645	77·3
1959	2,153	1,531	71·1
1960	2,063	1,508	73·1
1961	1,986	1,483	74·7
1962	1,930	1,457	75·5
1963	1,885	1,431	75·9
1964	1,849	1,426	77·1
1965	1,833	1,422	77·6
1966	1,836	1,444	78·7
1967	2,172	1,737	80·0
1968	2,226	1,806	81·1
1969	2,232	1,780	79·8
1970	2,137	1,709	80·0
1971	1,906	1,504	78·9
1972	1,802	1,413	78·9
1973	1,545	1,205	78·1

Sources: HMSO, Central Statistical Office, *Balance of Payments; Economic Trends*

long as Britain had no effective alternative and the United States was willing and able to provide the support.

The realisation that the strength of the dollar was not unlimited contributed to a deterioration in this area. In the sterling crises of the 1960s, the pound required massive help from European central banks as well as from the United States. The 1967 devaluation made it clear that the dollar could not support the pound indefinitely.[23] From the American perspective, there is a strong possibility that the 1967 sterling crisis and the subsequent devaluation of the pound, which did *not* lead to an immediate, extraordinary pressure on the dollar, signalled the end of the built-in, automatic link between the two currencies.

In retrospect, however, the British devaluation of 1967 appears to have been an early indicator of the precarious nature of the world monetary system. A series of crises followed, including the devaluation of the franc in 1969 and upward revaluations of the mark in 1969 and 1971. The significance of these developments was not missed in Europe, with serious discussions on monetary union being conducted and an initial agreement reached within the Community in 1971.

The United States, the pivotal point of the monetary system, was, as it turned out, not immune from mounting pressures either. Official acknowledgement of this came in August 1971, when President Nixon announced a new economic policy which included an import surcharge and a cessation of dollar convertability to gold. The Smithsonian Conference, four months later, produced a major realignment of world currencies and a follow-up agreement among Community members, the so-called 'snake in the tunnel' system.[24] The Smithsonian Agreement did not last however. The dollar has since been devaluated again, the pound has been floated and the 1973–74 oil crisis, with the resulting introduction of petrodollars as a world currency, has brought in more major participants with differing economic and political objectives.

While the American economy remains an important factor in the international system, the dominant position it once held, with its resultant ability to maintain 'special' bilateral relations, now seems a thing of the past. The British, as they continue to need economic assistance and support, will have to turn to international rather than bilateral mechanisms. A revised international monetary system may serve that end, or, alternatively, a European monetary union. A direct and exclusive link with the United States, however, is no longer an option.

In conclusion, in monetary as in trade relations, policy convergence is no longer a key to Anglo-American economic relations. The deterioration of the subsystem in these areas has been the result of both a changing international system and conscious choices by Britain and the United States.

Notes

[1] As used by John Pinder (see p. 27).

[2] For an examination of the early period see Richard Gardner, *Dollar–Sterling Diplomacy* (Oxford: Clarendon Press, 1956).

[3] For a review of this issue see David Calleo and Benjamin Rowland, *America and the World Political Economy* (Bloomington and London: Indiana University Press, 1973).

[4] See Miriam Camps' discussion of these negotiations in *Britain and the European Community*, chapter 8.

[5] See Joseph Kraft, *The Grand Design* (New York: Harper, 1962).

[6] 'Special Message to the Congress on Foreign Trade Policy, January 25, 1962', in *Public Papers of the President: John F. Kennedy, 1962* (Washington: Government Printing Office, 1963).

[7] The President requested the authority to cut tariffs to zero on commodities of which the United States and the Common Market together supplied 80 per cent of the world total. This list of items was significant only if Britain was included.

[8] See Max Beloff, *The United States and the Unity of Europe* (Washington: The Brookings Institution, 1963), p. 53.

[9] See George Ball's letter to Senator Paul Douglas in *Department of State Bulletin*, 18 March 1963. Ball seemed to be holding out the hope that the French veto of Britain's application was only temporary. American policy was to be patient and to continue to support the right kind of European unification.

[10] A series of pamphlets arguing for NAFTA was published by the Atlantic Trade Study in London. These include Maxwell Stamp Associates, *The Free Trade Area Option* (November 1967); Sir Roy Harrod, *Dollar Sterling Collaboration* (March 1968); Lionel Gelber, *World Politics and Free Trade* (July 1968); David Robertson, *Scope for a New Trade Strategy* (July 1968); and Geoffrey Williams, *Natural Alliance for the West* (June 1969).

[11] See the 'Javits Letter', *The Times* (21 February, 1967).

[12] Indeed, at this point all three British political parties were on record as favouring Common Market membership.

[13] *The Times* (7 October 1970). This British stand was enthusiastically received by officials of the Community (*The Times*, 8 October 1970).

[14] For a more complete discussion of this and related issues see Gian Paolo Casadio, *Transatlantic Trade: USA–EEC Confrontations in the GATT Negotiations* (Farnborough, England and Lexington, Mass.: Saxon House/Lexington Books, 1973).

[15] Ibid., p. 186.

[16] The American Ambassador to the European Communities, J. Robert Schaetzel, made this point to a group of European businessmen (*New York Times*, 13 February 1970).

[17] See, for example, *The Times* (29 September 1970).

[18] See John Marsh, *British Entry to the European Community – Implications for British and North American Agriculture* (London: British–North American Committee, 1971).

[19] Cmnd. 6003, para. 145.

[20] *European Community* (June 1974).

[21] Christopher Soames has repeated this point frequently, for example, to the European Parliament in April 1973 (*European Community*, June 1973).

[22] David Calleo and Benjamin Rowland, op. cit., p. 142.

[23] For a discussion of this point see Calleo, op. cit., p. 127.

[24] Under the Smithsonian Pact, it was agreed that the value of other currencies would be allowed to fluctuate against the dollar by plus or minus 2·25 per cent. This was the 'tunnel'. The Common Market nations agreed subsequently to limit the maximum gap between the value of their currencies to 2·25 per cent. This was the 'snake'.

c

6 Transactions: (1) Foreign Trade

The historical 'importance' of foreign trade to Britain is abundantly clear. On the one hand, trade can be seen in the most practical of terms. Commodities essential for survival have to be imported. This, in turn, requires the development of means to pay for the goods. The British have had to stress the significance of competitive export industries as well as the provision of 'invisible' services as revenue generators. Finally, the import of consumer goods can be seen as an indicator of an affluent society in Britain. Seen from this perspective, the patterns of British trade are not merely reflections of sentiment or of historical ties, but rather a measure of economic reality.

Of course, there is also a political dimension. Whether trade or the flag comes first, not all potential trading partners are equally available. While political affinity is obviously not a prerequisite for trading relations, there is probably a minimal threshold of mutual trust required before significant trade can be established. 'Significant' usually refers to the volume of trade, but the kinds of commodities involved might also be limited, for example, weapons or fuel. For, as diplomats realised long before theorists of integration, trade may lead to interdependence.

Trading arrangements may not always be balanced or calculated, but may instead be imposed. Even in a colonial system, however, different patterns of trade may develop.[1] The development of either a mercantile or a free trade system is not automatic, but being in a position to make the choice may be of considerable economic significance, as the nineteenth-century British experience would suggest.

Trade, as a measure of economic strength, as an indicator of interdependence, and as a mark of world role, is politically 'important'. Thus, if it is assessed carefully, the statistical record of British trade can tell a great deal about Britain's position in the world. The note of caution is deliberate. Such figures have been used to prove everything and nothing, often in good faith. However, following the general premise of this study that a range of factors needs to be examined, several different views of British trade with the European Community and the United States are offered here.

Looking at total trade with the United States and with the European Community, the patterns are mixed. Overall trade with both of these partners has risen sharply, with gross figures higher for both exports and imports with Europe than with the United States. (See Tables 6.1 and 6.2.) Total British imports increased between 1958 and 1974 by 503 per cent. Meanwhile, imports from American sources increased by 538 per cent compared with a figure of 1,077 per cent for imports from the original six member countries of the Common Market. In relative terms, the Community increase was 305 per cent of that from the United States.

Table 6.1

United Kingdom foreign trade: imports and exports, 1958–74 (£ million)

	Total	From/to US	Percentage from/to US	From/to EEC	Percentage from/to EEC
Imports					
1958	3,833·5	353·4	9·2	537·9	14·2
1959	4,086·6	373·5	9·1	564·9	14·0
1960	4,655·3	570·9	12·3	670·2	14·6
1961	4,546·4	492·3	10·8	691·0	15·4
1962	4,627·7	483·9	10·5	724·1	15·8
1963	4,983·4	508·0	10·2	790·8	16·0
1964	5,696·1	650·2	11·4	940·8	16·6
1965	5,751·1	671·4	11·7	994·7	17·3
1966	5,949·4	720·2	12·1	1,103·5	18·5
1967	6,436·7	812·1	12·5	1,264·0	19·6
1968	7,897·5	1,065·6	13·3	1,567·2	19·8
1969	8,315·0	1,132·4	13·5	1,610·9	19·4
1970	9,036·8	1,173·6	13·0	1,822·8	20·1
1971	9,834·0	1,095·1	11·1	2,105·8	21·4
1972	11,138·0	1,179·4	10·6	2,726·2	24·5
1973	15,854·0	1,622·0	10·2	4,189·0	26·4
1974	23,116·8	2,253·6	9·7	6,331·2	27·4
Exports					
1958	3,249·8	299·8	9·2	448·0	13·9
1959	3,422·8	392·4	11·5	508·8	14·7
1960	3,647·6	354·6	9·7	563·0	15·3
1961	3,796·0	320·1	8·4	661·7	17·3
1962	3,904·6	361·0	9·3	767·2	19·8
1963	4,211·1	379·8	9·0	874·3	21·1
1964	4,411·6	402·2	9·1	899·5	20·6
1965	4,728·0	493·7	10·4	904·8	20·0
1966	5,047·0	621·1	12·3	957·0	19·9
1967	5,028·8	610·3	12·1	963·7	20·0
1968	6,175·9	871·6	14·1	1,195·9	20·2
1969	7,337·6	903·4	12·3	1,526·0	20·8
1970	8,062·8	943·2	11·7	1,754·4	21·8
1971	9,181·0	1,074·6	11·7	1,926·2	21·0
1972	9,746·0	1,207·4	12·4	2,230·8	22·9
1973	12,455·0	1,512·9	12·1	3,073·9	24·7
1974	16,494·0	1,770·0	10·7	4,255·2	25·8

Source: HMSO, Central Statististical Office, *Annual Abstract of Statistics*

Similarly, on the export side both the American and European totals have risen at a faster rate than overall British exports, the Community total again being higher. The figures are: for all exports, 408 per cent; to the United States, 490 per cent; and to the Six, 850 per cent. The increase of the last-mentioned was 259 per cent of the American amount.

One means of comparing relative 'importance' in the trade sector is to examine the share of the total British market which both the United States and the Common Market had. For imports, the percentage from the Six in 1971 was 21·4 per cent of the British total. This was up 7·2 per cent from 1958 and the percentage had risen every year but one since 1959. Britain signed the Treaty of Accession in January 1972, and the figures since then have been

Table 6.2

Foreign trade with the enlarged Community, 1967–74
(as a percentage of total UK foreign trade)

	Exports	Imports
1967	26·5	26·5
1968	27·0	26·0
1969	28·1	25·8
1970	29·3	27·0
1971	28·3	29·6
1972	30·1	31·5
1973	32·3	32·7
1974	33·4	33·4

Source: European Community
Information Office

more striking. The share of imports from the Six rose to 24·5 per cent in 1972, to 26·4 per cent in 1973, and to 27·4 per cent in 1974, i.e. an increase of six percentage points in three years. If one uses the Community of Nine for calculations, then the 1974 total is 33·4 per cent.

The figures for imports from the United States show a distinct contrast. The 1974 share of the British market was 9·7 per cent, an increase of only one half point from 1958. Moreover, that figure represented a steady decline from the peak of 13·5 per cent in 1969. Thus the American total share of British imports in 1974 was only 35·6 per cent of the Six's share, and was down from 65·7 per cent in 1958.

The pattern for exports was not as steady, but the results are similar. The portion of exports to the Six in 1971 stood at 21 per cent of the British total, a rise of 7·1 points from 1958. Yet the percentage actually declined from 1963 to 1967 and did not regain the 1963 level until 1970. However, since the

Accession Treaty, there has been another sharp rise, up to 25·8 per cent in 1974.

Exports to the United States as a percentage of the British overall figure fluctuated in the first five years, then rose sharply until 1968, when they were up 4·9 per cent from 1958 and 5·7 per cent from the low mark of 1961. From that high point, however, the American share of the British export market has moved generally downward. The 1974 figure of 10·7 per cent was only 1·5 percentage points more than the 1958 figure.

In comparing shares of British trade, the Community has therefore been more 'important' throughout the period since 1958. The gap between UK–US and UK–EEC trade has widened appreciably, however. There has been a noticeable spurt in UK–EEC trade since membership was attained, with a concurrent decline in the relative 'importance' of trade with the United States.

Figures 6.1 and 6.2 examine British trade with the United States and the European Community from a different approach. They trace the yearly percentage change in British exports and imports to both partners as well as the annual change in the British total. As is to be expected, the lines representing changes in total exports and in total imports are more nearly horizontal, denoting the less drastic nature of change from year to year. The difference in both the export and the import graphs between the American and the Community line is striking.

For imports, the EEC graph until 1970 generally approximates the total British import picture, growing at a quicker rate but not dramatically so. Steep increases are evident in each of the years since 1970. United States imports, on the other hand, fluctuated widely, actually decreasing in three years and rising very sharply in three others. On the export side, the changes in total exports to the United States rarely came close to the overall figures, decreasing in three years – 1960, 1961 and 1967 – and being far in excess in four other years – 1959, 1965, 1966 and 1968. Exports to the Common Market rose at a constantly higher rate than the total growth rate until 1964. From then on they were less than the overall rate of increase until 1967. After 1967, these exports increased at a more rapid rate than the British total in all but one year. For both imports and exports, the very steep rise after 1972 is noteworthy. It can thus be seen that Common Market membership has led to a marked expansion of British trade.

There is another way in which the question of international trade should be examined. The increased 'importance' of the European Community to British trade and the relative stagnancy of Anglo-American trade have already been established. Yet how 'important' has British trade been to her two partners?

Table 6.3 shows the UK share of total exports and imports for both the Common Market and America from 1958 to 1972. As the figures indicate,

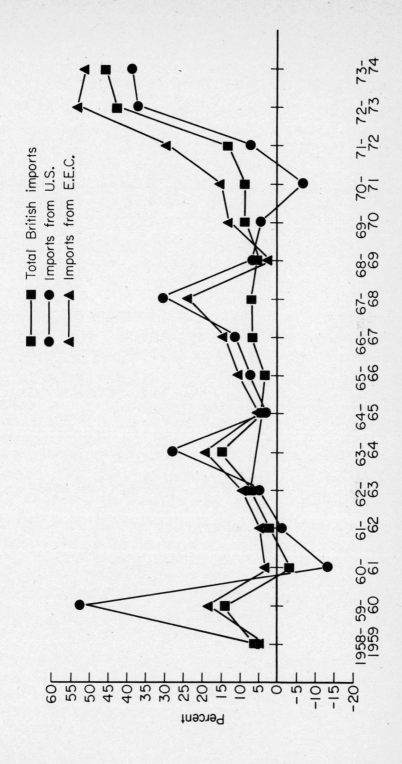

Fig. 6.1 Annual changes in UK imports

59

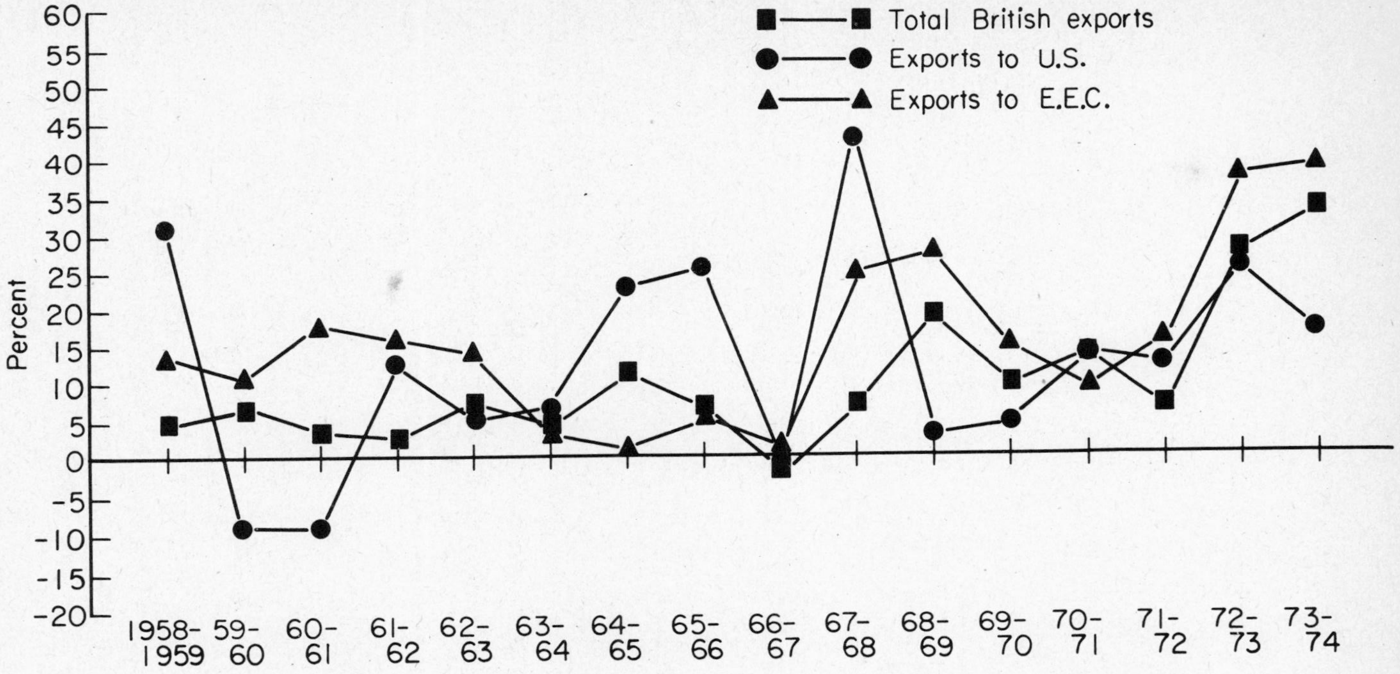

Fig. 6.2 Annual changes in UK exports

Table 6.3

The importance of the United Kingdom as a trading partner, 1958–72

	United Kingdom share as percentage of			
	EEC imports	EEC exports	US imports	US exports
1958	5·6	6·5	6·7	5·5
1959	5·6	6·2	7·5	5·0
1960	5·4	6·2	6·8	6·9
1961	5·8	5·9	6·1	5·6
1962	6·1	5·8	6·1	5·0
1963	6·2	5·7	6·3	5·0
1964	5·7	6·0	6·1	6·0
1965	5·6	5·8	6·6	5·9
1966	5·4	5·9	6·6	5·7
1967	5·2	6·2	6·4	6·2
1968	5·0	5·9	6·2	6·6
1969	4·7	4·4	5·9	5·5
1970	4·5	4·1	5·9	5·5
1971	4·4	4·5	5·5	5·4
1972	4·5	5·1	5·4	5·3

Sources: Figures based on statistics compiled from the Statistical Office of the European Community, *The Common Market: Ten Years On; Basic Statistics of the Community;* and United States Department of Commerce, *Survey of Current Business*

the UK percentage of Common Market trade actually dropped in the period up to 1970. Thus, while previous statistics indicated that both British exports and imports to the Community were rising, this table demonstrates how the Community totals rose at an even faster rate. The UK share of Common Market imports did rise until 1963, but after that it steadily declined. On the export side, the 'importance' of British trade was at a peak in 1958 and, with fluctuations, decreased in subsequent years. Again, for both exports and imports, there was an increase in apparent anticipation of British membership in the Community. In the case of the United States, the figures show no consistent pattern until recent years, in which there has been a steady decline.

Although British trade with the Six rose at a slower rate than did total Community trade, it is possible to modify this observation (see Table 6.4). Common Market trade from 1958 onwards steadily became more concentrated within the Community. Whereas imports from non-Community members accounted for 70·4 per cent of total imports in 1958, that proportion had dropped to 44·6 per cent by 1972. A similar trend held for exports, where the extra-Community percentage fell from 69·4 per cent in 1958 to 50·2 per cent in 1972. This pattern was the result of the creation of a customs union among the Six. After 1972, Britain was a member of that customs union.

Against these developments, British trade with the Community managed to rise slightly as a percentage of extra-Community imports. The gain of 1·2 per cent of the total import market was complicated by a decline from the peak of 10·1 per cent in 1963. In the case of EEC exports (British imports), the British share rose to a peak of 11 per cent in 1967 and then dropped sharply before increasing again prior to membership. Thus Britain managed to hold her own by this standard, but without any significant increase. Tables 6.3 and 6.4 would therefore seem to verify the impact of the institutional barrier on Britain prior to 1973. The spurt in British trade with her European partners after that date is evidence of the same point.

Volume of trade and comparative shares of total trade are not the only relevant measures. While those dimensions relate to commodity needs and to interdependence, an examination of Britain's economic strength and competitiveness with its accompanying financial implications requires additional figures.

One set of figures concerns trade balance. Trade deficits are not new: they predominated even in the nineteenth century when Britain was the industrial leader of the world. Nevertheless, factors such as the size of the deficit, how it is distributed, and whether other earnings provide an adequate surplus, are all matters of concern.

Table 6.5 lists the total British trade deficit and balance with both the United States and the European Community. While the UK did have trade surpluses with each of these trading partners on two occasions, the basic pattern has been a deficit. Moreover, there are some clear historical trends. Up to 1965, the British had a more favourable balance with the Six in all but two years. Since then, the reverse has been true. This last pattern is particularly significant in view of the growing concentration of British trade in Europe. Thus, for the period 1972–74, the Six accounted for roughly one-third of the total British deficit. Figures for the Community of Nine are even higher.

What such figures call into question is Britain's ability to compete economically within the European Community. Whereas the proportions were somewhat haphazard in earlier years, the share of the deficit from the Common Market has consistently exceeded the share of British total trade which the Community represents in the last four years on the table, at just the time when the British are deliberately moving toward Europe and anticipating economic stimulation from the experience.

A 1974 study reinforces this impression. Noting that almost three-quarters of the increase in imports between 1963 and 1972 was attributable to manufactured goods, L. F. Campbell-Boross and Ann D. Morgan of the National Institute of Economic and Social Research examined the performance of British industry in foreign trade.[2] They rated competitiveness by comparing

Table 6.4

The United Kingdom and extra-Community trade, 1958–72

	Extra-EEC imports as percentage of total	UK share	Extra-EEC exports as percentage of total	UK share
1958	70·4	8·0	69·4	9·4
1959	66·7	8·8	70·4	9·2
1960	65·7	8·2	65·9	9·5
1961	63·6	9·1	63·4	9·3
1962	62·5	9·8	57·5	9·6
1963	61·1	10·1	53·5	10·1
1964	59·8	9·5	53·9	10·6
1965	58·3	9·6	55·3	10·3
1966	57·3	9·5	54·7	10·5
1967	56·0	9·3	57·4	11·0
1968	54·0	9·2	57·0	10·7
1969	51·9	9·1	51·8	8·6
1970	51·6	8·8	51·5	8·0
1971	49·9	8·9	50·6	8·9
1972	44·6	9·2	50·2	10·2

Source: See Table 6.5

Table 6.5

United Kingdom trade deficits, 1958–74 (£ million)

	Total deficit	Deficit with US	US deficit as percentage of total	Deficit with EEC	EEC deficit as percentage of total
1958	583·7	53·6	9·2	89·9	15·4
1959	663·8	+18·9	Surplus	56·1	8·5
1960	1,007·7	216·3	21·5	107·2	10·6
1961	750·4	172·2	22·9	29·3	3·9
1962	723·1	122·9	17·0	+43·1	Surplus
1963	772·3	128·2	16·6	+83·5	Surplus
1964	1,284·5	248·0	19·3	41·3	3·2
1965	1,023·1	177·7	17·4	89·9	8·8
1966	899·3	99·1	11·0	146·5	16·3
1967	1,405·3	192·7	13·7	300·3	21·4
1968	1,723·5	182·0	10·6	371·3	21·5
1969	986·0	220·9	22·4	84·9	8·7
1970	988·8	230·4	23·3	68·4	6·9
1971	653·0	20·5	3·1	179·6	27·5
1972	1,392·0	+28·0	Surplus	485·4	34·9
1973	3,390·0	109·1	3·2	1,115·1	32·3
1974	6,622·8	483·6	7·3	2,076·0	31·3

Source: HMSO, Central Statistical Office, *Annual Abstract of Statistics*

changes in the ratio of the value of exports to the value of imports. Their results, shown in Table 6.6, demonstrate a pattern which they regard as unsatisfactory and disturbing for Britain's economic prospects.

An assessment of these different trade figures suggests several conclusions. The two most direct ones are that Britain has declined in economic competitiveness and that she has become much more closely linked with the European Community. The dimensions of both these trends are quite clear.

Table 6.6

Competitiveness of British export industries

	Export/import ratio, 1963	Average*				
		1964–67	1968–69	1970–71	1972	1973
Chemicals	1·8	88·6	82·7	84·0	82·4	79·1
Metals and manufactures	3·1	86·3	68·3	67·5	54·3	43·4
Engineering	2·6	74·0	66·8	67·6	64·8	52·5
Electrical goods	3·3	71·4	53·5	50·8	37·5	28·3
Transport equipment	14·9	63·2	46·3	32·1	16·3	14·1
Textiles	1·8	91·7	79·3	79·6	67·1	63·8
Leather, fur, clothing and footwear	0·8	112·3	121·8	120·8	96·5	79·6
Wood, paper and related industries	0·6	95·1	92·0	96·8	86·9	74·1
Rubber and other	2·3	84·3	78·6	84·7	68·9	58·6
Total	2·5	82·5	71·8	70·5	58·2	49·0
Total all manufacturing (SITC 5–8)	2·1	82·1	70·3	72·8	64·5	56·0

* Indicator of competitiveness: 1963 = 100

Source: L. F. Campbell-Boross and Ann D. Morgan, 'Net Trade: A Note on Measuring Changes in the Competitiveness of British Industry in Foreign Trade', *National Institute Economic Review*, no. 68 (May 1974), p. 81

The implications are less certain. One question is whether the two patterns are related. Additionally, what do these developments imply in terms of Britain's future?

It is certainly true that both the concentration of trade with Europe and the trade deficit increased sharply after Britain chose to become a member of the European Community. The period since 1972 has been a difficult one for Britain. In fact, though, several factors other than Common Market membership have to be considered. The dramatic rise in the price of some essential commodities, principally oil and food, has been costly and probably unavoidable. Indeed, the food costs might have gone up even more for the British if they had not been members of the EEC.

Moreover, those two trends were both evident well before 1973. For many British officials they have indeed been related. Economic difficulties provoked interest in Community membership. This observation, of course, does not rule out the possibility that membership in the Common Market has increased the economic problems facing Britain for, in the short term, that does seem to have been one effect of membership.

The long term impact depends on more than just foreign trade. Nevertheless, it is both a key indicator and significant in and of itself. What European Community membership provides is an opportunity, nothing more. There is no rule which prevents Britain from becoming the depressed area of Europe. In evaluating the prospects, however, the initial record of membership may not be the best standard.

A key to economic activity is planning and continuity. Throughout the period of British membership, the issue of a long term role has been debated. The possibility of withdrawal was not dismissed until 1975. A clear commitment to participation in the Common Market might, however, increase the *possibility* of sustained economic development.

One large trade deficit item is oil. Payment problems here have affected the entire economy. If, as anticipated, the deposits of North Sea oil become available in significant quantities, one barrier will be removed, or at least lowered. It seems highly doubtful that North Sea oil will overnight transform Britain into a prosperous nation. It might, however, give the country enough momentum so that the economy can start generating real growth again. The analogy of the take-off point for economic growth in an underdeveloped nation seems appropriate here.

Yet the key factor is probably internal. Britain's trade performance is affected by domestic political and social considerations as much as by economic ones. Just as industrialists require a degree of certainty before making economic commitments, a consensus on the kind of society that Britain is to be has to precede any fundamental economic revitalisation. It is this factor, discussed in greater detail elsewhere, which has to be understood in conjunction with the international economic system before Britain's trade prospects can be comprehended.

Britain will succeed within the European Community, her trade will prosper, and her economy will be competitive, if a sense of national unity develops. One of the frustrations of much of the postwar period has been that the prospects for fostering a consensus have been stifled by the lack of tangible opportunities. Once the old basis for an economic role was gone, uncertainty and disunity increased. The process has become a vicious circle. Breaking out of it is still not assured, but neither is it impossible.

Notes

[1] See the discussion of this point in Calleo and Rowland, op. cit., pp. 20–32.

[2] L. F. Campbell-Boross and Ann D. Morgan, 'Net Trade: A Note on Measuring Changes in the Competitiveness of British Industry in Foreign Trade', *National Institute Economic Review*, no. 68 (May 1974).

7 Transactions:
(2) Direct Overseas Investment

The benefits of international direct investment have long been argued.[1] At the same time, they have become an increasing reality of international economic life. Though the terms of the debate have not changed significantly since 1958, the patterns of foreign investment undoubtedly have.

As Table 7.1 indicates, Britain has not ignored the attraction of overseas investment. With respect to the two international subsystems under study, three patterns stand out. First, British annual investment between 1958 and 1965 was greater in the EEC than in the United States. This was no doubt the result of both the desire to circumvent the newly erected trade barriers of the Common Market and a recognition of the growth potential of the new economic union. From 1965 to 1970, with both of these factors continuing to operate, the level of British investment flow was maintained. However, during the period after 1965, the most striking trend was the increase in investment in the United States. British business responded to a prosperous American economy and to a need for diversified economic holdings. Another incentive was the example of the success of American business in overseas investment. Finally, there was a dramatic increase in direct British investment in the Community after 1970, although the American total also remained high.

A second aspect is shown in Table 7.1, namely the earnings on overseas investment. These represent the pay-off and are crucial to Britain's precarious balance of payments situation. In all but one of the years shown, the total earnings on overseas investment exceeded the net outward flow. This was true for all but three years in the case of investment in the United States, but was only so three times with respect to investment in the EEC. Still, after years of relative stagnation, the earnings on European investment did rise by 160 per cent between 1967 and 1968, prompting the Board of Trade to observe that 'It looks as though earlier investment in this area is at last bearing fruit'.[2]

Nevertheless, since the early 1960s, the growth rate on investment earnings from the United States has been quite high, and the total earnings from 1958 to 1972 were significantly more than from Common Market investment – £891·2 million as against £687·5 million. It is clear, then, that the economic benefits of this link with America were of continuing 'importance' for the British and showed no signs of diminishing.

Table 7.1

United Kingdom outward investment, 1958–72 (£ million)

	Net annual investment		
	Total	In US	In EEC
1958	146	10·7	8·0
1959	196	16·0	16·0
1960	250	15·7	22·0
1961	226	21·1	26·4
1962	209	10·2	29·2
1963	236	11·4	39·9
1964	263	31·3	36·7
1965	308	22·5	32·1
1966	276	41·7	50·5
1967	281	51·5	29·9
1968	410	84·0	76·0
1969	549	54·0	125·4
1970	546	134·0	93·2
1971	675	129·0	287·0
1972	731	105·0	241·5
	Net annual earnings		
1958	195	17·1	10·0
1959	238	20·2	18·0
1960	258	18·2	15·0
1961	249	19·4	19·8
1962	274	22·4	19·6
1963	330	38·4	21·1
1964	370	42·3	12·9
1965	400	48·6	19·1
1966	429	67·9	25·3
1967	438	72·5	24·7
1968	568	86·0	65·0
1969	650	94·0	83·0
1970	710	99·0	101·0
1971	717	108·0	104·0
1972	915	137·0	149·0

Sources: Board of Trade, *Board of Trade Journal* (7 August 1964, 9 May 1969, 6 April 1971); Department of Trade and Industry, *Trade and Industry* (13 June 1974)

The question of inward investment has also been controversial. While investment may be a link of interdependence, there has also been an awareness that it could lead to domination by the investing nation. The British have been vocally very concerned about the 'American invasion'. A *Financial Times* editorial in 1959 responded to fear of United States domination through investment takeovers thus:

In fact, however, there is considerable evidence that American investment has been of great advantage to the British economy. . . . Certainly, the British should not pretend that American investment endangers the national interest when the only rational fear would be that the Common Market will drain off too large a part of the investment that might otherwise have come to us.[3]

Table 7.2 shows the level of annual direct foreign investment in the United Kingdom since 1958 and the totals from the United States and from the

Table 7.2

United Kingdom inward investment, 1958–72 (£ million)

	Net annual investment		
	Total	From US	From EEC
1958	87	62·1	1·0
1959	146	97·2	9·0
1960	135	84·3	4·0
1961	236	186·3	17·2
1962	130	94·5	2·5
1963	160	103·7	9·7
1964	162	116·4	19·3
1965	197	150·9	14·8
1966	195	154·7	8·9
1967	170	94·0	46·7
1968	274	217·3	25·4
1969	319	204·4	35·1
1970	354	222·8	50·7
1971	445	283·4	35·1
1972	363	244·8	34·3

	Net annual earnings		
1958	95	70·6	9·0
1959	136	96·6	11·0
1960	137	102·0	7·0
1961	128	100·2	6·8
1962	134	105·9	5·5
1963	168	134·3	6·7
1964	203	153·5	18·8
1965	235	180·1	14·8
1966	204	152·0	12·8
1967	216	153·5	16·8
1968	329	245·3	21·1
1969	308	231·4	14·0
1970	360	264·0	24·3
1971	390	286·1	31·0
1972	523	375·7	51·3

Sources: see Table 7.1

European Community. These figures clearly demonstrate the continuing predominant position of American investment. Indeed, up to 1967, the European figure was relatively meagre.

A similar pattern of United States pre-eminence held for earnings from inward investment. The American portion was close to 75 per cent of the total earned in Britain. Further, from a strictly financial point of view, the British had a negative balance in total investment transactions with the United States, with an earnings ratio of roughly one to three. Similarly, United States earnings from investment in Britain exceeded the annual inward flow in all but three years. These figures suggest that American investment had, and continues to have, an enormous impact on the United Kingdom. By contrast, European investment has been relatively 'unimportant'. Even British membership in the EEC has not yet had a substantial impact on investment flow.[4]

Direct investment as a policy area

All this adds up to a picture of highly 'important' economic relations with the United States. Some would even call it dependence. It is from this point that two interesting and sometimes contradictory elements of British policy come. On the one hand, there was an expressed desire to achieve greater independence from the American colossus, perhaps by organising within a European context. Thus Harold Wilson made this a major theme of his 1967 campaign to join the Common Market and demonstrated his 'European-ness' in expressing these thoughts in a speech to the Council of Europe:

> Let no one here doubt Britain's loyalty to NATO and the Atlantic Alliance. But I have also always said that loyalty never means subservience. Still less must it mean an industrial helotry under which we in Europe produce only the conventional apparatus of a modern economy, while becoming increasingly dependent on American business for the sophisticated apparatus which will call the industrial tune in the 70's and 80's.[5]

Yet the desire to eliminate American 'industrial helotry' did not mean that the British wanted to do without United States investment or expertise. Indeed, as the *Financial Times* had warned in 1959, the greatest fear seemed to be of losing American investment to the Common Market. Thus the Wilson Government in its 1970 White Paper assessing the economic impact of Common Market membership on Britain made the following observation:

> Linked with the question of growth is the degree to which the United Kingdom will in future attract overseas investment – particularly from

the United States. In addition to its benefits to the reserves, this has been of considerable benefit to the United Kingdom economy in several ways; in providing jobs (particularly in development areas), in its contribution to exports and in the dissemination of technology and management techniques. If the United Kingdom remained outside the Community, it is likely that American investment in the Six would be stimulated at the expense of the much smaller and less rapidly growing United Kingdom market. If on the other hand the United Kingdom entered it is likely that we would attract substantially more American investment to this country than if the United Kingdom remained outside.[6]

While Britain had 12·5 per cent more American investment in 1958 than the six nations which formed the Common Market, that balance shifted rather quickly. As Table 7.3 shows, the total value of US investment in the EEC surpassed the total in Britain in 1963 and grew at a significantly higher rate after that. A good deal of attention was drawn to the subject of American investment in Europe by Jean-Jacques Servan-Schreiber's *The American Challenge*.[7] Although a number of his observations seem questionable today, the overall phenomenon of American investment described by him has continued. Moreover, Western Europe has continued to attract an increasing portion of the total. Indeed, by 1973, the Six plus Britain accounted for nearly

Table 7.3

Value of United States direct investment abroad (end of the year)

	Total ($ million)	Investment in UK		Investment in EEC	
		$ million	Percentage	$ million	Percentage
1958	27,255	2,147	7·9	1,908	7·0
1959	29,827	2,477	8·3	2,208	7·4
1960	32,778	3,231	9·9	2,644	8·1
1961	34,684	3,523	10·2	3,104	8·9
1962	37,225	3,824	10·3	3,722	10·0
1963	46,686	4,172	8·9	4,490	9·6
1964	44,343	4,550	10·3	5,398	12·2
1965	49,328	5,123	10·4	6,304	12·8
1966	54,711	5,657	10·3	7,584	13·9
1967	59,267	6,101	10·3	8,405	14·2
1968	64,756	6,703	10·4	8,992	13·9
1969	70,763	7,158	10·1	10,194	14·4
1970	78,178	7,996	10·2	11,774	15·1
1971	86,198	9,007	10·4	13,605	15·8
1972	94,337	9,582	10·2	15,720	16·7
1973	107,268	11,115	10·4	19,294	18·0

Source: United States, Department of Commerce, *Survey of Current Business*

29 per cent of American overseas investment, twice the proportion of 1958.

While trends are quite clear, their effect is less certain. The impact of overseas direct investment is the subject of much controversy on *both* sides of the Atlantic. As the British White Paper indicates, there are numerous benefits to the recipient country. Perhaps most telling today is the access to the technology and management techniques which accompany American investment. These can provide a shortcut in time as well as financial savings for various kinds of industrial development. Christopher Layton, an early student of this subject, suggests another benefit to Europe:

> American corporations with interests in different European countries have an immense interest in the stability and strength of Europe, and in good relations between the two continents. . . . Direct investment enhances America's interest in the security of Europe, strengthening a commitment which most European Governments regard as vital. It is a cement of unity for the Atlantic world.[8]

At the same time, many Europeans say they are unhappy about American economic hegemony. There is the fear that, in a vital situation, an American-controlled company might make a decision detrimental to European interests. What is disturbing to some in Europe is not the magnitude of American investment so much as the sectors in which it is concentrated. The United States has come to dominate in the advanced technological fields, leaving the more conventional areas to the Europeans.[9]

Nevertheless, whatever their fears, the fact is that the Europeans have made little material effort to check the flow of American dollars and the resulting American influence. This observation has held true as much for France and other members of the European Community as it has for Britain.

With respect to Britain's relationship with the Community, the American investment trend should have eliminated one of the early issues of contention between Britain and the Six: that British membership of the Common Market would lead to a backdoor takeover of Europe by the United States. The dollars poured in the front door and nobody rushed to close it.[10]

To understand the dilemma involved for Europeans in the question of American investment, it is necessary to consider first some of the implications of modern technology. A great deal has been written about the Atlantic technological gap.[11] Both the suggestion that the American lead in advanced technology springs from the considerable government research and development expenditure in the defence field[12] and the claim that the gap is really a managerial one[13] have some merit. Yet these observations have not led to a reversal of the American domination of the frontier technologies.

The first question to be answered is what difference does it make. Why could not the Europeans concentrate on those fields in which they have a competitive advantage – such as metallurgy, chemicals, or the peaceful use of atomic energy – and not concern themselves with those areas in which there is a gap?

The reply to this question is, in economic terms, an old one. Economic benefits are associated with innovation. Servan-Schreiber argues that 'modern power is based on the capacity for innovation, which is research, and the capacity to transform inventions into finished products, which is technology.'[14] The competitive advantage rests with the firm which can produce innovative products. America is in the position of innovator in such key fields as computer technology, electronics, and the aerospace industry, while the Europeans struggle to refine old processes and concentrate on conventional products. The constantly accelerating rate of scientific discovery makes this pattern likely to continue.

From this perspective, the impact of American investment can be seen more clearly. The United States has a lead in the advanced technological sector. As a result of this lead, American businessmen are able – with resources, expertise, and organisation – to gain control of developing advanced industries in Europe. This is the key issue. Few people really care if the British eat American cornflakes or brush their teeth with American toothpaste. However, in sectors related to both national security and the economic competitiveness of the country, there are objections.

Alternatives are available. One would be to cut off American investment. Since this would also cut off access to the associated modern technological benefits, European nations have been reluctant to do this. Furthermore, this approach would have to be a coordinated one: otherwise, a French decision to ban IBM, for example, would merely result in the factory being moved across the border to Belgium.

The other alternative tackles the problem more directly, but, because of its far-reaching political implications, has not been successfully implemented. This is European technological collaboration.

The logic of this approach is very attractive to many Europeans, some of whom see it as a step towards building a united Europe and others of whom believe it is the only way to prevent complete industrial domination by the United States. This has certainly been one of the main attractions of the European Community for the British.[15]

Full-scale European technological collaboration would deal directly with the problem of scale and its three component parts, research, production and marketing. The Europeans have always been very envious of the resources available to both the United States government and to large American firms. It is these resources which enable the conducting of far-flung research

73

projects and the conversion of the findings of those projects into marketable commodities. There is no question that the cost factor is a highly important one in advanced industries. The third factor in the equation is the size of the available market. American firms have the assurance of a tariff-free market of over 200 million people.[16]

The upsurge of large multinational corporations – not all American-based – seems to be an indicator of the direction of future development. What has been lacking in Europe thus far is a willingness to accept the full implications of technological collaboration. This is ultimately a political consideration. Up to now, the coordination of separate national policies in Europe has been uneven.

In an operational sense, a number of problems can be identified. There has been a tendency to treat each project separately, rather than as part of an overall European technological programme. Collaboration has not taken place on all levels, but rather on narrowly prescribed programmes. The emphasis on receiving benefits commensurate with the national cost input on each separate project has been a major stumbling block to more innovative and imaginative efforts. Specific collaboration in the military field, with emphasis on the aerospace industry, will be discussed in Chapter 11, but the overall record of European technological cooperation has been mixed. Efficiency has not been high, but some projects have been undertaken on a bilateral or multilateral basis beyond the capability of any individual European nation acting alone. Trans-European contacts and discussions have been initiated, but no lasting groundwork has been laid for systematic collaboration in the future.

Both the pressures for, and the potential benefits of, technological cooperation still exist, but there has not yet been a demonstration of the needed political will.[17]

Up to now, therefore, European progress in this sector has remained largely in the realm of the potential. Similarly, so has the 'importance' of the European subsystems for the British.

Notes

[1] For studies concerned particularly with Britain see W. B. Reddaway et al., *Effects of UK Direct Investment Overseas* (Cambridge: Cambridge University Press, 1967); J. H. Dunning, *American Investment in British Manufacturing Industry* (London: George Allen and Unwin, 1958); J. H. Dunning, *Studies in International Investment* (London: George Allen and Unwin, 1967); and M. D. Steuer and Associates, *The Impact of Foreign Direct Investment on*

the United Kingdom (London: HMSO, Department of Trade and Industry, 1973).

[2] *Board of Trade Journal* (8 April 1970).

[3] *Financial Times* (22 April 1959).

[4] The lag in official statistics complicates an assessment of this area. Nevertheless, previous trends do seem clear.

[5] Harold Wilson in a speech to the Council of Europe's Consultative Assembly (23 January 1967).

[6] HMSO, *Britain and the European Communities: An Economic Assessment*, Cmnd. 4289, para. 68. The Commission of the European Communities agreed that the United Kingdom would probably attract more American investment if she joined the Common Market (*Opinion*, op. cit., para. 109). For a different conclusion see Douglas Jay, *After the Common Market* (London: Penguin, 1968), p. 59. There are, in fact, early indications that US companies have significantly increased their investments in Britain as a result of EEC membership (*The Sunday Times*, 8 June 1975).

[7] Jean-Jacques Servan-Schreiber, *The American Challenge* (New York: Atheneum, 1968).

[8] Christopher Layton, *Trans-Atlantic Investment* (France: The Atlantic Institute, 1966), p. 30.

[9] For a discussion of this development with respect to British industries see J. H. Dunning, *Studies in International Investment*, p. 315.

[10] Harold Wilson, in replying to de Gaulle's second veto in 1967, observed that at least the British had kept *their* computer industry independent.

[11] See, for example, the series of studies published in 1967 by the Institute for Strategic Studies, *Defence, Technology and the Western Alliance*. Also Arnold Kramish, *Atlantic Technological Imbalance: An American Perspective* (London: Institute for Strategic Studies, 1967); John Diebold, 'Is the Gap Technological?', *Foreign Affairs* (January 1968); and the *Report of the Conference on Transatlantic Technological Imbalance and Collaboration*, sponsored by the Scientific-Technological Committee of the North Atlantic Assembly and the Foreign Policy Research Institute, University of Pennsylvania, and held at Deauville, France (25–28 May 1967).

[12] See Robert Pfaltzgraff, Jr, Chandler Rajaratnam, and Thomas White, 'Comparative Research and Development Expenditures and Atlantic Technological Imbalance', a paper presented at the Deauville Conference.

[13] Diebold, op. cit.

[14] Servan-Schreiber, op. cit., p. 276.

[15] For example, Harold Wilson proposed a European Technological Community. See his Guildhall speeches, November 1966 and November 1967.

[16] For a discussion of the importance of certainty in modern industrial

production see John Kenneth Galbraith, *The New Industrial State* (New York: The New American Library, 1967).

[17] For a more thorough discussion of this issue see Roger Williams, *European Technology: The Politics of Collaboration* (London: Croom Helm, 1973).

PART II

MILITARY RELATIONS

8 British Defence Policy: Orientation and Capabilities

> Where metaphysicians once interminably disputed how many angels
> could dance if need be on the head of a pin, they now, in and outside of
> Westminster, debate defence (*The Times*, 2 March 1964).

British defence policy in postwar years has been one of the most debated, and
most maligned, topics of public discussion. One commentator in the late 1960s
observed that the 'major landmarks of the past ten years have been cancellations of weapons projects and growing enfeeblement of cold war forces.'[1]
Those trends have, if anything, accelerated since then.

The subtitle of L. W. Martin's excellent paper on British defence policy for
the Institute for Strategic Studies is most apt: 'The Long Recessional.'[2]
Two key factors stand out in this process. In the first place, Britain entered
the postwar era from a position of recognised world power status. Even if she
were decidedly the third of the Big Three, she could be mentioned in the same
breath without embarrassment. This lofty vantage point has been a difficult
one from which to climb down. Secondly, the effects of economic weakness
have been felt in a less dramatic but perhaps more agonising way than military
defeat might have been. British defence policy has had to be made and carried
out in the face of reduced economic capability.

Of course, the state of the economy has always been a factor. Indeed, as
Neville Brown has observed, 'The over-extension of military resources – or
the pitting of 'short bayonets against long odds' – has happened so frequently
as to become almost a national tradition.'[3] Still, the constraints have been
greater than many people recognised, and this has resulted in problems.

The record of Britain's relative decline in economic power was given in
Chapter 2. The specific impact of this on defence can be readily seen. Table 8.1
shows defence expenditure from 1952 to 1974. Although the gross defence
budget has continued to increase, the total as a percentage of GNP has
declined steadily since 1953. This trend has occurred at a time of soaring costs
for defence hardware. And, in 1974, after a lengthy defence review, the Labour
government announced that future defence spending would be reduced to
4·5 per cent of GNP.[4] The explanation was clearly in terms of economic constraints rather than changing perceptions of the military situation.

Table 8.1

United Kingdom defence expenditure, 1952–74

	Expenditure (£ million)*	Expenditure as a percentage of GNP
1952	1,561	10·0
1953	1,681	10·0
1954	1,569	8·8
1955	1,567	8·2
1956	1,615	7·8
1957	1,574	7·2
1958	1,591	7·0
1959	1,589	6·6
1960	1,657	6·5
1961	1,709	6·3
1962	1,814	6·4
1963	1,870	6·2
1964	2,000	6·1
1965	2,091	6·0
1966	2,153	5·7
1967	2,276	5·8
1968	2,332	5·5
1969	2,303	5·1
1970	2,444	4·9
1971	2,800	5·1
1972	3,272	5·4
1973	3,481	5·5
1974	3,800	5·2

* Current prices

Source: Stockholm International Peace Research Institute, *World Armaments and Disarmament: SIPRI Yearbook 1974* (New York: Humanities Press, 1974)

A second table, showing comparative defence efforts, suggests that the reduction in British expenditure is bringing the UK into line with her major Western European allies, but at a level lower than that of the United States. (See Table 8.2.)

Of course, defence expenditure, taken by itself, means little. What makes it significant is the scope of commitments it is intended to cover. For the British, the list has been rather imposing. The major undertaking in Europe has been membership of NATO. This was reinforced by assurances made in the Western European Union (WEU) Treaty of 1954 to maintain four divisions in Europe.[5]

Outside Europe, until the latter part of the 1960s, Britain was also heavily committed. The United Kingdom maintained extensive military forces in both the Persian Gulf and South East Asia. This East of Suez presence was

Table 8.2

Comparative defence expenditure, 1952–74 ($ million)*

	UK	France	West Germany	US
1952	6,958	4,469	3,207	70,100
1953	7,263	4,994	2,565	71,978
1954	6,694	4,217	2,603	62,370
1955	6,379	3,922	2,968	58,850
1956	6,215	5,118	2,816	59,645
1957	5,859	5,312	3,407	60,825
1958	5,726	4,905	2,535	60,858
1959	5,719	5,004	4,047	61,192
1960	5,893	5,158	4,375	59,554
1961	5,886	5,316	4,612	62,008
1962	5,997	5,513	5,854	67,241
1963	6,057	5,418	6,580	66,280
1964	6,274	5,568	6,306	64,096
1965	6,256	5,658	6,232	63,748
1966	6,201	5,821	6,108	76,043
1967	6,394	6,133	6,351	87,730
1968	6,257	6,127	5,637	90,103
1969	5,864	6,045	6,142	86,274
1970	5,850	6,014	6,188	77,854
1971	6,120	6,010	6,638	71,776
1972	6,682	5,952	7,080	72,087
1973	6,509	6,274	7,290	68,586
1974	6,175	6,202	6,833	68,446

* 1970 prices and 1970 exchange rates

Source: Stockholm International Peace Research Institute,
World Armaments and Disarmament: SIPRI Yearbook 1974
(New York: Humanities Press, 1974)

seen by the British not only as a historical commitment, but also as an area in which they were uniquely equipped to make a contribution to international peace and stability.

A non-geographical area of defence policy has been the development and maintenance of a nuclear deterrent. This has been considered a vital aspect of British defence policy, both as a contribution to Western defence and as a measure of Britain's military standing in the world. While the British developed their own nuclear capability in the 1950s, they then found it necessary in the 1960s to seek assistance for their delivery systems. The rapid growth of modern technology has provided a major challenge in this area.

The nature of these three commitments has meant a serious stretching of Britain's resources.[6] The British attempted for a time to maintain a global military role with a decreased capability. An unwillingness to recognise the imbalance between resources and commitments has been the dilemma of British defence policy. The result has been a constant effort to juggle resources to hold on to the full domain of British influence.

In the manpower field, the pressure was intensified by the 1957 decision to eliminate National Service after 1960. In shifting to a volunteer army, the total of British military personnel fell by over 160,000 men between 1960 and 1970.

Table 8.3 shows the deployment of British forces for that period, as less manpower was stretched over the same global area. Allocation of resources is one test of priorities. While troop deployment required expressing preferences, the figures also show that the juggling of resources continued. The competing priorities suggested by these figures are examined in later chapters.

The conflict between re-ordering priorities and financial constraints is also demonstrated in Table 8.4, a list of aircraft and missiles cancelled by the British government between 1952 and 1965. Britain invested over £300 million in aircraft projects that were eventually cancelled, a sum which represented 20 per cent of total research and development expenditure in the aerospace field. However, the impact of the cancellations has not merely been financial. The time lost in development and production of replacements and the effect upon defence planning are also significant. Indeed, of 37 military aircraft projects initiated since 1945, only 22 were completed. Moreover, the cancellations were not, for the most part, the result of technological difficulties, but, rather, of economic limitations and political uncertainty about the proper role of Britain's forces.

Analysts have seen a number of different decisions – the development of a nuclear deterrent, the WEU commitment, the ending of National Service – as making inevitable an eventual scaling down of Britain's total commitments. Yet such a step was doggedly resisted. Changes have come in Britain's defence policy, but reductions have seemed more the result of necessity than of choice.

The main concerns of British defence policy have been the nuclear deterrent, NATO, and the East of Suez presence. The United Kingdom's military capability did not dictate emphasis on these policies, but it has determined how effectively they could be pursued. Increasingly, pressures have developed to choose among these three areas. In the case of the last two, the determination of a global versus a regional military orientation has made the element of choice more explicit.

From this perspective, Britain's military relations with the United States and with the European Community can be seen more clearly. In the first place, interaction in these crucial policy areas has been of great 'importance' to the British. The extent of cooperation and assistance within each of the subsystems has been a major factor in augmenting or diminishing Britain's military capability. Thus, with respect to policy interaction, a number of questions are relevant.

82

Table 8.3

Deployment of United Kingdom forces ('000 men, as at 1 January)

	1960	1961	1962	1963	1964	1965	1966	1967	1968	1969	1970
Navy:											
United Kingdom	55·4	51·2	50·7	52·0	54·0	53·1	55·4	53·7	55·9	53·2	52·3
West Germany	—	—	—	—	—	—	—	0·1	—	—	0·2
Mediterranean	5·8	4·8	4·1	3·4	2·9	2·9	2·2	2·1	1·9	1·7	1·3
Middle East	0·2	0·9	1·0	—	—	1·2	1·4	1·2	0·3	0·3	
Far East	2·0	1·8	2·1	2·8	2·9	3·1	4·3	4·4	5·0	4·5	4·3
Afloat and other	37·8	39·5	39·2	37·6	38·3	40·7	37·8	37·7	35·1	33·7	28·9
Total	101·3	98·3	97·1	96·9	99·2	100·9	101·1	99·2	98·2	93·5	87·0
Army:											
United Kingdom	153·0	118·3	103·4	96·9	94·4	94·1	95·4	102·3	107·8	105·4	98·3
West Germany	52·9	54·7	55·4	53·5	54·4	54·2	56·1	55·7	56·6	53·0	53·1
Mediterranean	18·8	16·8	11·6	9·1	11·1	10·5	10·1	9·3	8·8	8·0	7·8
Middle East	9·5	9·3	10·0	10·9	13·6	17·4	17·4	12·2	4·7	5·3	30·3
Far East	41·5	41·7	37·0	36·4	38·5	43·4	39·5	37·3	33·5	29·7	
Other	13·4	18·1	16·3	12·8	9·9	5·2	2·5	1·7	4·5	0·4	4·2
Total	289·2	258·9	233·7	219·7	221·9	224·8	221·0	218·6	216·0	201·8	193·8
Air Force:											
United Kingdom	125·0	122·8	114·3	109·3	100·4	92·2	88·0	87·3	91·7	87·4	86·8
West Germany	13·1	12·1	9·6	9·2	8·9	8·8	8·7	7·7	7·1	6·6	6·9
Mediterranean	12·0	11·3	10·7	9·9	9·5	9·7	9·8	8·9	7·8	7·8	8·5
Middle East	5·4	6·3	6·3	7·0	7·6	7·7	7·9	7·4	3·4	3·4	10·2
Far East	7·6	7·2	7·0	7·1	8·4	8·6	10·3	10·1	9·5	8·3	
Other	2·4	2·2	1·9	2·1	3·1	5·0	4·7	3·9	2·7	2·6	1·3
Total	165·5	161·9	149·8	144·6	137·9	132·0	129·3	125·3	122·2	116·2	113·7
Total all services	556·0	519·1	480·6	461·2	459·0	457·7	451·4	443·1	436·4	411·5	394·5

Source: personal correspondence with United Kingdom Ministry of Defence

Table 8.4

Aircraft and missiles cancelled before going into service, 1952–64

	Estimated expenditure (£ million)	Cancellation date
Transport aircraft:		
Brabazon transporter	6·45	February 1952
Princess flying boat	9·1	May 1954
Vickers military transporter	4·0	December 1955
Orion turbo-prop aero engine	4·75	January 1958
Rotodyne helicopter	11·0	February 1962
Operational aircraft:		
DH fighter	2·5	May 1952
Developed Hawker Hunter	0·14	July 1953
Swift fighter	22·0	February 1955
Swift photo-reconnaissance and fighter	0·3	June 1955
Swift crescent-wing research fighter	1·6	December 1955
Avro rocket interceptor	1·0	September 1955
Thin wing Javelin all-weather fighter	2·3	June 1956
Fairey supersonic fighter	0·15	March 1957
Supersonic bomber (including engine)	2·05	March 1957
Naval Interceptor	3·2	December 1957
Scorpion rocket engine	1·25	February 1959
Spectre rocket engine	5·75	October 1960
P.1154	25·0	February 1965
HS.681	4·0	February 1965
TSR.2	195·0	April 1965
Missiles:		
Guided bomb with television eye	3·1	June 1954
Vickers flying bomb	0·7	September 1954
Air-to-ship guided bomb	0·9	March 1956
Air-to-air missile with radar guidance	7·5	June 1956
Longe-range surface-to-air guided weapon	1·5	May 1957
Heavy anti-tank missile	2·4	September 1959
Blue Steel Mark II	0·825	December 1959
Bloodhound Mark III	0·6	March 1960
Blue Streak ballistic missile	84·0	April 1960
Low-level surface-to-air guided weapon	0·8	December 1961
Medium range surface-to-surface missile	32·1	August 1962
Skybolt air-to-surface ballistic missile	27·0	December 1962
Medium Range Swingfire (anti-tank missile)	0·234	November 1964

Expenditure figures have been extracted from records extending over a number of years and may not all be on an identical basis. For more recent cancellations, estimates have been given. Both sets of figures should be regarded as approximate.

Source: *Hansard*, House of Commons (14 April 1965), cols. 206–7

(1)   What patterns[7] were prevalent in the past?
(2)   Did the British receive adequate support to achieve their objectives, or were they forced to modify their policies?
(3)   Did new patterns develop as the result of British shifts in orientation?

Concerning transactions, one key problem is identifiable. The main material concern of the British in international military transactions has been the acquisition of weapons. Indeed, the shift from self-sufficiency to a need for other nations' help in this sector was one measure of Britain's diminished capability. As the weapons acquisition problem was recognised, alternative solutions were considered. This process can be evaluated in terms of transactions within each of the subsystems. In addition, interaction between the two subsystems is observable since Britain has had options in each.

Britain's changing defence capability is the key background factor for examining her military relationships with the United States and with the European Community. The evolution within each of these two subsystems is therefore the next focus of attention.

Notes

[1] Richard Rosecrance, *Defense of the Realm* (New York: Columbia University Press, 1968), p. 250.

[2] L. W. Martin, 'British Defence Policy: The Long Recessional', *Adelphi Papers*, no. 61 (London: Institute for Strategic Studies, November 1969).

[3] Neville Brown, *Arms Without Empire* (London: Penguin, 1967), p. 14.

[4] *New York Times* (4 December 1974).

[5] Western European Union Treaty, Protocol no. 11, Article 6.

[6] See Michael Howard, 'Britain's Defenses: Commitments and Capabilities' *Foreign Affairs*, vol. 39, no. 1 (October 1960).

[7] See page 2 for 'pattern of relations' in the definition of international subsystems.

9 Military Policy: (1) Britain and Europe

It was the lack of a commitment to Europe in the defence field that de Gaulle most directly attacked in 1963 when he vetoed the first British application to the Common Market.[1] The British Prime Minister, Macmillan, seemed to confirm this attitude in his speech to the House of Commons acknowledging and defending a 'special relationship' with the United States in the military field.[2] Eventually British officials became aware that defence matters constituted one test of 'European-ness' for them.[3] This, in turn, affected the pattern of military relations within the British–European subsystem.

Regional policy

Of course, Britain has been allied with the other nations of Western Europe for many years. This was affirmed in the North Atlantic Treaty, of which Britain was one of the leading champions. Indeed, British governments throughout the entire period since NATO was founded have emphasised their deep commitment to it and their recognition that NATO has to be kept strong to forestall any threat to Western Europe.

However, these attitudes toward NATO did not, by and large, gain the British much credit for being 'good Europeans'. Three reasons mitigated against this. For the British, NATO meant, first and foremost, a vehicle for tying the United States to Europe and for ensuring that the American commitment remained permanent and unwavering.[4] In a sense, this relationship gave Britain a chance to exercise influence above that which her military strength might have warranted. In addition, such a role tended to differentiate Britain from the other European members of NATO.

The second criticism from the European viewpoint was an operational one. While acknowledging that NATO should receive first priority, the British tended to argue that the more immediate risks to peace really existed outside Europe, and that it was in those areas that Britain had a unique contribution to make. Harold Macmillan spoke of the 'fundamental difference' between Britain and her continental allies in the following terms:

We have, of course, to make a contribution, and we are making it loyally to the NATO forces, but we have obligations also in many other parts of the world, and the defence of the free world, and indeed, the survival of the free world, is assisted by our efforts in some of these more distant areas.[5]

A third concern was the nature of Britain's abstract view of NATO. The United Kingdom was opposed to supranational organisations but had been willing to participate in intergovernmental ones. This was the distinction, for instance, between the European Defence Community, which Britain refused to consider, and the Western European Union, which Britain helped to organise. NATO represented a slightly different case. While there are some supranational features incorporated into the NATO structure, the presence of the United States has provided definite checks upon NATO becoming a link in an integrative movement.[6]

In the first place, the United States has been one of the most reluctant nations to give up sovereignty to a supranational organisation. In the case of NATO, it has been more a question of American domination than of American sharing. To be sure, the contribution of the United States has been, in fact, essential. But, at the same time, the United States has held all the key cards and has not had to sacrifice decision-making authority.

Secondly, NATO was not seen as contributing to European integration. The advantage of NATO for Europeans has been simple: deterrence. The political case is not so clear. To the extent that a desire for greater independence and for the ability to compete represent motivating factors for European integration, the presence of the United States in NATO has disqualified that organisation.

Thus, British support for NATO did not necessarily demonstrate a European defence orientation. The preceding remarks should indicate that an approach to Europe through NATO has severe built-in limitations in any case. As a result, the willingness of Britain to adjust her position on regional versus global commitments has been a major concern.

There was no immediate change of position following the de Gaulle press conference in January 1963. A look at the Labour Party, which came to power in the October 1964 elections, shows that the stand on NATO was bipartisan and, if anything, held even more strongly by Labour than by the Conservatives. Denis Healey, later Minister of Defence and not considered pro-European, nevertheless strongly favoured the link with NATO. Not long before taking office he noted:

(But) I believe that Britain's effective voice on the continent will depend as much on diplomatic influence in Washington as on her military contribution in Germany, and the former may be substantially increased by a readiness to share the American burden outside Europe and to integrate her atomic forces in a common NATO pool.[7]

The first major test of Labour's views on NATO came with the debate over the multilateral force (MLF) proposal in 1964. Although the British had serious reservations about the idea, they were not willing to oppose the United States on the matter. Their equivocal attitude was demonstrated by their suggested modification, an Atlantic Nuclear Force (ANF). In essence, the MLF case demonstrated a British reluctance to concentrate their military efforts within a European context.[8]

Similarly, the first Labour Defence Statement, in February 1965, repeated a familiar theme:

> It is therefore pointless to tie up resources against the risks of a prolonged war in Europe following the nuclear exchange.
>
> The British contribution is paramount in many areas East of Suez. . . . Our presence in these bases, our Commonwealth ties, and the mobility of our forces, permit us to make a contribution toward peacekeeping in vast areas of the world where no other country is able to assume the same responsibility.[9]

The 1966 Defence Statement indicated that financial constraints would force the British to impose some limitations on global commitments.[10] Still, this was a rather negative moving toward Europe. A more positive step was taken in the Supplementary Statement on Defence published in July 1967. This was in the midst of the second British application to join the European Communities and marked an overt effort to link the defence field with other areas of European cooperation.

> The security of Britain still depends above all on the prevention of war in Europe. We, therefore, regard it as essential to maintain both the military efficiency and political solidarity of the North Atlantic Treaty Organization. For this purpose, we must continue to make a substantial contribution to NATO's forces in order to play a part in the defence of Europe and to maintain the necessary balance within the Western alliance. *This contribution will become even more important as we develop closer political and economic ties between Britain and her European neighbours.*[11] (Author's italics.)

Although the second application led to another rebuff by de Gaulle, the British continued to stress their military commitment to Europe. This was a key ingredient in their diplomatic offensive after the second veto.

In the first place, Britain emphasised again her belief in the connection between the military sector and other areas of European integration. British defence statements started to sound like testaments to the country's 'European-ness'. The supplementary statement in 1968 argued that 'In defence, as in every other field, the first and fundamental assumption on which the Government believes that Britain must base her future policy is the need for closer unity in Europe.'[12] The 1969 statement was even more explicit: 'The essential feature of our current defence policy is a readiness to recognize that political and economic realities reinforce the defence arguments for concentrating Britain's military role in Europe.'[13]

Britain did not, however, limit herself to these general affirmations of faith. An effort was made to present specific material examples of Britain's 'European-ness'. The British noted that the hastened withdrawal from East of Suez would enable them to offer to increase the forces available to NATO.[14] This the British were able to announce at a time when the Canadians were withdrawing some of their NATO contingent.

In addition, the British took the lead in arguing for a European defence identity within NATO. One vehicle for this was the regular informal meeting of European Defence Ministers before the NATO Council meeting, the so-called Eurodinners. Denis Healey's initiative was important in establishing these contacts.

The 1970 Defence Statement continued the British effort to find specific means of creating a European identity:

> The key to greater progress in European defence cooperation is closer collaboration between the European military staffs in developing and harmonizing their tactical doctrines. . . . The United Kingdom has substantially developed its contacts with the European allies to this end in regular bilateral staff talks.[15]

Thus, as one example, the Germans and the British collaborated on a paper setting down guidelines for the tactical use of nuclear weapons.[16] The two nations jointly developed a computerised model of a land battle in Europe at Britain's Defence Operations Analysis Establishment in Surrey. A second example was the number of Europeans studying at the Imperial Defence College from 1970 onwards, eight out of a total of seventy-two in the first year.

These changes did not mean, however, that the British wanted to cut off Europe from the United States in the defence field. Denis Healey, writing in 1969, made this quite clear.

> As all American leaders have stressed, nothing would do more to encourage the United States to maintain its necessary commitment than the sight of the European countries working together effectively within the alliance.[17]

In a general sense, NATO combined the European and American options of defence policy for the United Kingdom. In official statements NATO had always been given a high priority, but, in the late 1960s, there was a definite change of emphasis by the British in their attitude towards this policy area.

The coming to power of the Conservative Party in June 1970 did not reverse this pattern, but it did lead to a slowing down of the change in regional orientation. Edward Heath's government continued to emphasise the priority of NATO and Europe, but it declined to eliminate the British presence East of Suez.

A Supplementary Statement on Defence Policy in October 1970, highly critical of the previous Labour government for weakening Britain's military strength,[18] spoke of maintaining the primary commitment to NATO, but added that 'there are also serious threats to stability outside the NATO area. Britain will be willing to play her part in countering them' within her resources.[19] Specifically, a Five-Power defence arrangement with Australia, Malaysia, New Zealand and Singapore was established. Reversing the Labour decision to withdraw from East of Suez, the plan envisioned military consultation as well as the presence of several thousand British troops.

Heath's Conservative government, which was undoubtedly highly pro-European, nevertheless hung on to the image of a British global presence, albeit limited, even as Britain became a member of the European Community. In defence matters, the Conservatives were not anti-European: indeed, they pushed on in all the areas pursued by the Labour government. The informal talks among European ministers in NATO were formalised as the Eurogroup.[20] The British were active participants in the establishment through the auspices of the Eurogroup of a European Defence Improvement Programme, by which defence contributions were increased. The Conservatives maintained the British involvement in technological collaboration in the defence field.[21] Moreover, Edward Heath, while not expecting immediate results, was more willing to talk about the possibility of nuclear cooperation in Europe than were his Labour predecessors.[22]

Yet, the Heath Government continued to feel that

> British interests and responsibilities are not confined to the NATO area. Britain's political and trading interests are world-wide and they can flourish only in stable conditions. She must be willing, therefore, to play her part, though on a scale appropriate to her resources, in combating threats to stability outside Europe.[23]

After the February 1974 election, the new Labour government initiated a lengthy review of British defence policy. In deciding to reduce the amount spent on defence, Labour returned to its policy of phasing out the British presence East of Suez. The conclusion of Defence Minister Roy Mason, in announcing the pull-back from Singapore and Hong Kong, that 'we are no longer able to police the world',[24] could just as well have been reached many years before. The reductions did not, however, affect the 55,000 troops stationed in West Germany under NATO.

The move from global involvement to an exclusive European concentration, now apparently irreversible, has been difficult. Despite both the economic constraints on globalism and the symbolic political value of a European defence orientation, British governments have been slow to give up totally those 'wider interests' which distinguished the British from other Europeans. The cost of that reluctance, in economic, military and political terms, has been heavy.

In terms of defence policy in Europe, Britain started from a position of strength. Today her ability to make a substantial contribution is less certain. Thus, while Anglo-European defence relations have become much closer and more 'important', the impact of the shift has not been so dramatic.

Nuclear relations

De Gaulle and Macmillan were in total agreement on one point in January 1963: that Britain had a special nuclear relationship with the United States. However, they differed in assessing its significance for Anglo-European relations.

De Gaulle saw the British deterrent as firmly interlocked with America's – and apparently Robert McNamara shared this view. In making their application to the Common Market, the British did not see military (and in particular, nuclear) matters as being part of the new Europe. Although Nora Beloff reported that some British officials in 1962 were interested in eventual Anglo-French cooperation,[25] the overall record suggests that this interest was not very strong.

And, indeed, there were some logical reasons for this. In the first place, there was no real expectation that the European Community would be able to function effectively in the military sector in the foreseeable future. Although some saw such cooperation as coming eventually, even the most optimistic regarded it as being many years in the future. Secondly, the British had a very satisfactory nuclear partnership with the United States, a termination or modification of which would have involved enormous complications. The British certainly enjoyed greater benefits from the alliance with the United States than they would have from one with France. In addition, some delicate legal questions would have arisen regarding the transfer of nuclear technology which the United States had made available to Britain.

The sticking point in this issue was de Gaulle. His desire to restore French grandeur intensified the French position. Almost from the beginning of his term of office, he insisted upon an increased status for France.[26] While French military strength was being developed, de Gaulle determined to achieve his objective by diplomacy. A distinctive aspect of that diplomacy was the personality of de Gaulle himself: he succeeded in making himself a world figure, perhaps a personification of the France which he hoped to mould.

For de Gaulle, the procedure was almost as important as the goal. French nuclear capability could in no way be diluted. Thus, he did not want a French force that was closely linked to an American one, nor one that was the product of American help.[27] De Gaulle's consciousness of being a world historical figure also interposed itself in his relations with other countries. Thus, he would not be the 'demandeur' even when he wanted something. As a result, many issues were never raised nor given the chance to be resolved.

So it was with nuclear relations between France and Britain. De Gaulle's general views were well-known. Yet, the British managed to avoid an explicit examination of this question until it was too late,[28] until after de Gaulle's veto of Britain's Common Market application. As has been mentioned, the British, up to 1963, were not inclined to make a new nuclear arrangement with the French anyway. Moreover, there is no assurance that it would have been possible to come to an arrangement with de Gaulle on this issue. His citing of it may have been only a rationalisation. Nevertheless, the British were vulnerable on this issue.

For essentially the same reasons which were pertinent before the veto, the British did not attempt to make a nuclear 'deal' in 1963 to reverse the decision. Miriam Camps argues that the key factor was a feeling that collective action in the defence field by Europe was still a long way off.[29] However, this assessment really misses the point of a deal. Clearly, what the British had to come to terms with in 1963 was not reality but rather de Gaulle. However, as already started, there was no inclination by British officials at that time to revise their nuclear arrangements.

The Labour government seems to have come to office with a similar point of view. In 1964 they were not, of course, favourably disposed to joining Europe. Thus Harold Wilson could reject the idea of a separate European deterrent, saying it would weaken and divide NATO.[30]

As Labour's views on Europe changed, visibly in 1966, the implications of collaboration with Western Europe were reassessed. Still, it was the Conservatives, and particularly Edward Heath, who took the lead on the nuclear issue. At Harvard in early 1967, Heath proposed that the British and French nuclear forces should be pooled to form a joint deterrent which would be held in trust for Europe.[31] The exchange between Wilson and Heath in the House of Commons on this subject in May 1967 indicated that the Prime Minister still retained reservations about Anglo-French nuclear collaboration.[32]

Still, events demonstrated that the British had managed to defuse the nuclear issue of its political disadvantages. The basis for de Gaulle's veto of the second British application in 1967 was monetary, not military. Although the Labour government had not gone as far as the Conservative Opposition on the nuclear issue, their willingness to accept in principle the implications of participating in the European movement lessened their political vulnerability on this matter.

The British continued to emphasise the military field within the Anglo-European subsystems after the second veto. With respect to nuclear relations L. W. Martin notes that, in the two years following de Gaulle's second veto,

> British defence planners have taken advantage of their special access to nuclear information to take a lead in trying to develop a common European view on the important question of tactical nuclear weapons.[33]

Nevertheless, nuclear relations with Europe by 1970 were still not very 'important' for the British. A willingness to consider seriously the issue within the context of the subsystem represented a change from the early 1960s. However, that evolution, when compared with Anglo-American nuclear relations, was slight.

There was, in the context of the third set of British negotiations on Common Market membership, some talk of a European nuclear force being developed at some stage.[34] An alternative version was that the British should be willing to pool their nuclear technology as a 'price' for entry.[35] Actually, however, there seems to have been little official interest in collaboration at that time or since: for example, the French Defence Minister Michel Debré made it clear on numerous occasions that France was not inclined to pursue such a policy.[36]

Influential commentators, such as François Duchêne, have kept the discussion going on European nuclear cooperation, but with the recognition that nothing will happen soon. While arguing that defence collaboration is necessary if Europe is to influence rather than be shaped by the international environment, Duchêne acknowledges that 'a European nuclear force is as remote as the election of a federal European President.'[37]

Yet, if collaboration is distant, an awareness exists that nuclear relations and developments are important to Europe. The existence of NATO and the American deterrent has been seen as critical to European security. Historical events have demonstrated, however, that European control over security matters is slight. Soviet advances in nuclear capability raised doubt in many European minds about the credibility of American guarantees. Shifts in US defence policy and domestic debates about the American world role raise the same issue. The willingness of the United States and the Soviet Union to engage in nuclear summitry, while rational and.encouraging in some respects, also has an ominous side for the Europeans. As John Newhouse notes, the SALT talks have been the only major East–West transaction in which the European nations did not participate.[38] The first phase, in agreeing to limit ABM deployment, may have benefited the British and French nuclear forces,[39] but a second phase including agreement on Foreign Based Systems would have very different consequences.[40]

For Europe, the issues are as much political as military. The technological capability to develop and maintain a European nuclear force exists. On the one hand, however, such a step would imply a basic lack of confidence in American commitments. And, in addition, it would require a degree of political unity which has yet to be evidenced.

Moreover, time is a factor. A credible, independent European nuclear force cannot be developed quickly. Even if the French and British efforts are complementary,[41] consolidation would not be easy. Meantime, will the British and French be able to maintain their own national programmes? The British have avoided making a decision on the next generation of nuclear weapon systems.[42] Eventually, delay will give way to obsolescence. The basic dilemma, for Europe as a whole as well as for Britain, is deciding what kind of military role to play in the world.

Notes

[1] See his press conference comments on the Nassau Agreement (14 January 1963).

[2] House of Commons (30 January 1963).

[3] For instance, Harold Wilson observed that 'It was the Nassau Agreement that slammed the door of the Common Market in Britain's face' (*Financial Times*, 19 March 1966).

[4] See Ben Moore, *NATO and the Future of Europe* (New York: Harper, 1958), p. 61.

[5] *Hansard*, House of Commons (1 January 1963), cols. 959–60.

[6] For a discussion of this point see Francis Beer, *Integration and Disintegration in NATO* (Columbus: Ohio State University Press, 1969), p. 239.

[7] 'Defence: A Financial Times Survey', *Financial Times* (23 March 1964).

[8] This situation was somewhat ironical, since the British were resisting an American suggestion to give greater emphasis to their NATO role. Nevertheless, the global orientation remained paramount.

[9] HMSO, *Statement on the Defence Estimates 1965* (Cmnd. 2592, February 1965), paras 8 and 9.

[10] HMSO, *Statement on the Defence Estimates 1966: Part I, The Defence Review* (Cmnd. 2901, February 1966), para. 19. The key phrase was 'Nevertheless, to maintain all our current military tasks and capabilities outside Europe would impose an unacceptable strain on our overstretched forces, and bear too heavily on our domestic economy and on our reserves of foreign exchange.'

[11] HMSO, *Supplementary Statement on Defence Policy 1967* (Cmnd. 3357, July 1967), para. 1.

[12] HMSO, *Supplementary Statement on Defence Policy 1968* (Cmnd. 3701, July 1968), para. 73.

[13] HMSO, *Statement on the Defence Estimates 1969* (Cmnd. 3927, February 1969), para. 2.

[14] HMSO, Cmnd. 3701, para. 17.

[15] HMSO, *Statement on the Defence Estimates 1970* (Cmnd. 4290 February 1970), para. 39.

[16] Interview with Denis Healey, *Government Executive*, vol. 1, no. 10 (December 1969).

[17] Denis Healey, 'NATO, Britain, and Soviet Military Policy', *Orbis* (Spring 1969).

[18] HMSO, Cmnd. 4521, para. 2, *passim.*

[19] Ibid., para. 5.

[20] See 'Aspects of NATO: The Eurogroup', NATO Information Service (Brussels, November 1972).

[21] See the discussion of this on page 118.

[22] This point is examined in greater detail on page 93.

[23] HMSO, *Statement on the Defence Estimate 1971* (Cmnd. 4592, February 1971), para. 1. This same sentiment is repeated in the 1973 Defence Statement (Cmnd. 5231), para. 15.

[24] *New York Times* (4 December 1974).

[25] Nora Beloff, *The General Says No* (London: Penguin, 1963), p. 150.

[26] An early example was his 1958 memorandum proposing a three-power directorate for NATO composed of the United States, Britain and France.

[27] Indeed, there are indications that he could have made an arrangement to receive help from the United States. One instance was the offer of Polaris after the Nassau Conference. For a general discussion of this point see John Newhouse, *De Gaulle and the Anglo-Saxons* (New York: The Viking Press, 1970), p. 35.

[28] While reports of the Macmillan–de Gaulle meeting at Rambouillet in December 1962 vary, it seems that this issue was not examined directly. See Newhouse, *De Gaulle and the Anglo-Saxons*, p. 208; Nora Beloff, op. cit., p. 158; Camps, *Britain and the European Community*, p. 469.

[29] Camps, *European Unification in the Sixties*, p. 127.

[30] *Daily Telegraph* (17 November 1964).

[31] Edward Heath, Old World, New Horizons, *The Godkin Lectures at Harvard University, 1967* (Cambridge: Harvard University Press, 1970), p. 73.

[32] *Hansard*, House of Commons (9 May 1967). See also HMSO, *Statement on the Defence Estimates 1967* (Cmnd. 3203, February 1967), para. 16.

[33] Martin, op. cit., p. 18.

[34] See, for example, *The Times* (6 June 1970). Also Drew Middleton, 'There May be a Nuclear Marriage', *New York Times* (6 July 1969).

[35] The Commission of the European Community proposed this idea in reference to Euratom (*The Times*, 14 April 1970).

[36] *Washington Post* (16 June 1971).

[37] François Duchêne, 'The Strategic Consequences of the Enlarged European Community', *The Atlantic Community Quarterly*, vol. 11, no. 2 (Summer 1973), p. 208.

[38] John Newhouse, *Cold Dawn: The Story of SALT* (New York: Holt, Rinehart and Winston, 1973), p. 271.

[39] Andrew J. Pierre, 'The Salt Agreements and Europe', *The World Today*, vol. 28, no. 7 (July 1972) p. 286.

[40] Newhouse, *Cold Dawn*, p. 271.

[41] This point is discussed by Andrew J. Pierre, 'Nuclear Diplomacy: Britain, France, and America', *Foreign Affairs*, vol. 49, no. 2 (January 1971), p. 295. See also Paul C. Davis, 'A European Nuclear Force: Utility and Prospects', *Orbis*, vol. 17, no. 1 (Spring 1973), p. 127.

[42] Pierre, *Nuclear Politics* (London: Oxford University Press, 1972), p. 297, discusses the lack of planning for a successor to Polaris.

10 Military Policy: (2) Britain and the United States

The United States and Britain have common membership of NATO, SEATO, and the Security Council of the United Nations. In many respects the two nations have demonstrated similar outlooks toward international affairs. Both have been globally-oriented, nuclear powers. Both are used to playing a world role. Both have stationed large numbers of military forces overseas. Each has supported, in large measure, the role undertaken by the other.

Moreover, the scope, ease and informality of relations between British and American officials have been truly extraordinary in the field of interstate relations. Patterns of trust and habits of cooperation have developed over many years. While sharp differences of opinion have occurred, proponents of the 'special relationship' argue that, in a critical situation, the British and the Americans can always depend on each other.

The problem with such an analysis is that it is based on static factors. While a dependable ally is surely a desirable asset, both national interests and national capabilities change. Since 1945, a decline in British military strength was not the only observable change: both nations have modified their national goals and orientations. Inevitably, such developments have an effect on international alliances.

In fact, the persistence of the 'special relationship' surprised many. Both common interests and habits have played a part, but changes have nonetheless come, as interaction in main policy areas demonstrates.

Global cooperation

Both Britain and the United States have stressed the importance which they assign to NATO. Yet neither has limited its military activities to Europe; rather, both have agreed that they have a wider role to play. The main focus of this wider interaction has been Asia.

A joint presence in Asia was both a symbol of global partnership and a source of cooperation in the Anglo-American subsystem. The deterioration of that link has been somewhat ironical. As economic pressures mounted, British officials tried to avoid the temptation of cutting back their presence in Asia as a means of economising in their overall defence effort. In this they received considerable American encouragement.[1] As *The Sunday Times* noted, 'The Americans . . . appreciate the value of the Army's global efforts.'[2]

Yet the East of Suez commitment was a costly one. In the absence of a cutback in the scope of Britain's defence efforts, her resources were stretched ever thinner. The perception by Washington of a diminished capability on the part of the United Kingdom led to a decreased willingness to consult with Britain on military matters. Thus, despite a presence East of Suez and membership in SEATO, Britain was not represented at the 1966 Manila Conference on the Vietnam War. Similarly, in the case of the 1970 American invasion of Cambodia, the British were given no prior information.[3]

The relationship showed other signs of strain in this area. As the British ability to make a real contribution diminished, the United States started turning to this policy area as a test of British commitment to close Anglo-American relations. This latter tendency accelerated as the United States, increasingly involved in the last half of the 1960s in a war in South East Asia, found herself diplomatically at odds with her Western allies. In choosing to give verbal support to American involvement in Vietnam, Britain perpetuated the split between herself and other Western European nations.[4] And, ironically, the rewards were not great, as American officials considered the amount of support given to be inadequate.[5]

Moreover, the last half of the 1960s saw the start of a British withdrawal from Asia. A State Department official called the 1966 United Kingdom Defence White Paper a 'milestone' in Anglo-American relations. This document signalled the acceptance in Britain of a need to withdraw from a global position.[6]

A plan for an orderly pullout by the mid-1970s was announced in the Supplementary Defence Statement of 1967.[7] This timetable was greatly speeded up in January 1968 as part of the austerity measures which accompanied devaluation. The State Department expressed its official disappointment at these measures: 'We regret the British Government's announcement regarding its forces in South-east Asia and the Persian Gulf and the F-111 contract. . . . The United States has no plans to fill the gap left by Britain's accelerated withdrawal.'[8] There are indications that the American government, on a number of occasions, expressed its private disapproval as well.

Other symbols of Britain's sharing a global role with the United States diminished in number. Although Britain was involved in negotiations for the Nuclear Non-Proliferation Treaty, she was not a participant in the Strategic

Arms Limitations Talks. Rather, she was watching and waiting with the rest of Western Europe. The pretence of consultation was rapidly disappearing, as the Cambodian invasion demonstrated. While a commitment to NATO remained, it was coloured by an emphasis by the British on a European identity within the organisation.

These developments showed that the United Kingdom was finally giving up her attempt to play a global role. While this decision had been resisted for many years, the pressures in the end became too great. As global commitment has been a prerequisite for global partnership, the Anglo-American military alliance has declined in 'importance' for both partners. For the United States, Britain is no longer able to make a worldwide contribution. For the British, global policy has been assigned a lower priority and a regional defence orientation has been increasingly emphasised.

Nuclear relations

> Sometimes people talk, and sometimes complain of a special relation between Britain and the United States. This is a general phrase which is sometimes justified, or perhaps justified, by the very close understanding in certain fields, by similar methods of work and thought, and by the traditions which bind the two countries. But in the instance of nuclear power there was, indeed, a special arrangement which existed from the start and which has now been restored. In the atomic and nuclear field, there is a very full interchange between Britain and America of the results of our separate research. After all, we invented it together, and I cannot see that this is a grievance for our continental friends.[9]

The nuclear connection between the United States and Britain, the touchstone for de Gaulle's anti-Anglo-Saxon position of January 1963, was affirmed at Nassau in 1962. Yet these close ties went back much farther. As Harold Macmillan noted, the United States and Britain were involved in wartime nuclear cooperation, which was interrupted by the 1946 MacMahon Act.[10] The 1957 meeting of Macmillan and Eisenhower led to a 1958 amendment to that act which provided nuclear assistance for Britain. The level of cooperation increased considerably after that and, significantly, much of it was highly visible.

An agreement was reached in 1958 to place sixty Thor missiles in the United Kingdom.[11] Then, in 1960, when the British decided to discontinue development of the Blue Streak missile as a military weapon, the United States offered a replacement, the Skybolt. Some of the discussions which took place at that time reveal the closeness of Anglo-American cooperation in the nuclear field.

On the day of Defence Minister Harold Watkinson's announcement of the cancellation of Blue Streak, the Department of State confirmed that the United States and Britain had been holding talks for 'several months' on the possibility that the Skybolt missile would replace it.[12] The lack of reservations about making the missile available to the United Kingdom lent further credence to a 'special relationship'.

In his statement, Watkinson observed that 'the vulnerability of missiles launched from static sites, and the practicability of launching missiles of considerable range from mobile platforms, has now been established.'[13] British knowledge of mobile-launched missiles came from the American development of Skybolt and Polaris. The reference to the vulnerability of fixed-site missiles reflected an awareness of recent Russian tests of their ICBMs. American intelligence had been important in convincing the British of this new threat.[14]

Britain's chances of getting the Polaris missile were also widely discussed at this time. Watkinson told the House of Commons in June 1960 that 'The Polaris programme, thanks to the close and cordial relations between the United States and United Kingdom Navies, has had our naval personnel integrated in it almost from its inception.'[15] However, despite this the British decided not to accept Polaris at this time.

The specialness of these arrangements is shown in two ways. First of all, the United Kingdom was willing to become dependent militarily on the United States. Although this was not officially acknowledged, the need to rely on American supply of a delivery system made it inevitable, as the cancellation of Skybolt was to show in 1962. Significantly, Britain was willing to place national trust in the United States.

Likewise, the decision to make American nuclear equipment and expertise available to Britain represented a dramatic reversal of United States policy. Both Congress and the Atomic Energy Commission felt very protective towards all things nuclear. Thus the 1958 amendment and its subsequent implementation reflected an act of faith in the solidarity of Anglo-American relations. In Karl Deutsch's terms, a pluralistic security community was thought to exist.

A further exception was made for Britain during the Kennedy Administration. Secretary of Defense Robert McNamara, in a well-publicised speech, criticised the development of national nuclear forces.[16] His specific target was the French 'force de frappe', but lest there be any confusion, he issued a statement the following week saying that he had not been talking about the British deterrent.[17]

The visible highpoint of the nuclear 'special relationship' was the Nassau Conference in December 1962. In a strictly military sense, Nassau presented mixed results. Following an American decision to cancel the Skybolt missile, the decision was made at Nassau to offer the British the Polaris as a substitute.[18] This increased the effective life of the British nuclear deterrent and also showed the extraordinary closeness of Anglo-American military ties.

However, because the United States had some reservations about offering Polaris to the British, two qualifying provisions were made. First, an identical offer was made to the French. Although a willingness was expressed to negotiate arrangements to meet the special needs of the French,[19] de Gaulle pronounced the offer a sham and rejected it out of hand. While the transmittal of the offer may have been clumsy, it seems to have been genuine. The implications of nuclear partnership with the United States probably weighed more heavily with de Gaulle than the material and information which he would have received.

As a second point, the United Kingdom agreed to pledge her nuclear deterrent to NATO except in times of 'supreme peril' to Britain. Although de Gaulle did not think such an escape clause provided sufficient independence for France, the British considered that they had, by the inclusion of that phrase, preserved their sovereignty. From the American point of view, the British pledge to NATO was thought of as the first step toward solving the problem of nuclear sharing in the Atlantic Alliance.

The vehicle for this was to be the multilateral force (MLF), an idea first developed in the last days of the Eisenhower Administration. Henry Kissinger has called the MLF an 'attempt to implement the Grand Design without France and, if necessary, against it.'[20] To follow this line of reasoning, the original concept of a Grand Design of Atlantic Partnership had been rendered inoperative by Britain's exclusion from the European Community. In the military field, the historical relationship of American and Europe within NATO was coming into question. France's chosen independence on defence matters made her participation in an American-inspired reorganisation problematic.

If the MLF had been pursued vigorously, the question would have been to what extent France would have become isolated in other sectors as well. In fact, the idea never did win widespread approval,[21] not even from the British. Only when, in 1964, it seemed that the United States and West Germany were determined to go ahead with the MLF did the British express a willingness to participate. And even then they proposed their own variation, an Atlantic Nuclear Force (ANF).

Miriam Camps has argued that this reluctance reflected the fact that the British did not give overriding priority to the European relationship at that time.[22] It does seem that they did not consider defence matters, particularly of a nuclear kind, to be an integral part of their prospective relationship with Europe. However, more to the point, the British still believed in the special status of their own nuclear position.[23] Although facts might belie that belief, the British were still reluctant to give up all pretence of an independent nuclear force.

The MLF episode seemed to reinforce the point made at Nassau, that the semblance of an independent British nuclear force was a critical national objective. Accommodation with the United States was seen as necessary to that objective, while alternative arrangements were seen as threatening Britain's position. In the case of the MLF, however, the British attitude was maintained in spite of a contrary American position. This made the fantasy a bit harder to maintain.

Nuclear cooperation in the Anglo-American subsystem from the early 1960s onwards has been of a different order. The Polaris agreement was carried out and Britain has built a fleet of four missile-carrying submarines.[24] At this point in time, the British government has indicated that it is not interested in the next generation of missiles, the Poseidon.[25] The formal agreements on exchange of information and of nuclear material were extended in 1968 and 1969 and again in 1974. Thus, while nuclear cooperation has continued, there have been no new agreements nor any dramatic public demonstrations of a special relationship in this field after the 1962 Nassau Conference. The 'importance' of the United States to Britain in the nuclear area has continued only as the result of prior arrangements.

Two possible issues loom in the future. If the British and French were to move toward nuclear collaboration, would the United States invoke legal restrictions to transferring nuclear information? The fact that assistance has been offered to the French in the past may not be controlling. While some analysts have argued that British and American expertise is so intertwined in the nuclear programme that the restriction on transferrence is not practical or legally enforceable, the political consequences of acting in the face of American opposition would be serious. If the question arises, the American attitude is most likely to be based on the overall state of relations with Europe, economic and political as well as military.

The second issue involves the future of the British deterrent. The Polaris system will last into the 1980s. Britain has already decided not to request Poseidon as a replacement, but, as old-age and new technology begin to lessen the viability of the British nuclear forces, harder questions will have to be dealt with. Will the United States make the next generation of missiles available to the British? Will the British want them? Will they be able to afford them?

The answers are likely to come in an entirely different context for Britain than was the case with the Polaris agreement. Britian as a part of a fragmented European Community would have neither the resources nor the political will to pursue a nuclear role. In the alternative situation, if Britain were an active member of an integrating European Community, the decision on seeking the American system would be likely to be a joint one. An affirmative US response in those circumstances would strongly suggest the existence of a 'special relationship' between the United States and Europe rather than between the United States and Britain.

The special relationship

The term 'special relationship' has generally been used to refer to the military alliance between the United States and Britain. While this sector remained 'important' to Britain throughout the period of this study, some adjustment was clearly evident.

Nuclear cooperation continued unabated although no new agreements were concluded after 1962. The willingness of the United States to offer the Polaris as a substitute for the cancelled Skybolt was widely seen as proof of a 'special relationship'. After 1962, this sector was not seriously tested.

By contrast, in the other main aspect of military partnership, a shared global orientation, significant changes occurred. In the first place, Britain, from 1966 onwards, withdrew her presence East of Suez. As a result, the opportunities for close collaboration with the United States in Asia have greatly diminished. This area was thus reduced as a sector of 'important' relations within the Anglo-American subsystem.

In the second place, the nature of joint participation in NATO changed. The Atlantic Alliance remained central to British defence efforts and the role of the United States was essential to the strength of NATO. Nevertheless, Britain's orientation within the organisation was altered. Active collaboration at the European level was seen as 'important'. More significantly, the defence field was considered to be related to other sectors of European integration.

The hard fact is that a military alliance with the United States has meant military dependence on the United States. The 1960 Skybolt agreement made this the case with respect to the nuclear deterrent. For anyone who had missed the point, the cancellation of Skybolt by the United States in 1962 made it unmistakably clear. Moreover, Britain was also dependent in a psychological sense. The United States, as the overwhelmingly stronger partner, has been continually able to control the closeness of the alliance.

In conclusion it may be said that as Britain's military capability decreased, so did her favourable position with the United States. The reorientation of British defence policy was the result of an inability to maintain her former role. The United States remained essential to Britain's defence, but the basis for a 'special relationship' in this area has grown ever weaker.

Notes

[1] See, for example, Henry Brandon, *The Sunday Times* (18 July 1965).

[2] *The Sunday Times* (5 January 1964).

[3] As George Liska has noted, 'Information is the least exacting form of consultation' (Liska, op. cit., p. 85).

[4] *The Guardian* quoted 'a Member of the Government' on this dilemma: 'But it is the Government's attitude to the Vietnam war which has most clearly distinguished it around the world from other European Governments and has given rise to an unhappy strife within the Labour Party' (*The Guardian*, 1 October 1968). See also Anthony Sampson, *Anatomy of Europe* (New York: Harper and Row, 1968), p. 386.

[5] Louis Heren in *No Hail, No Farewell* (New York: Harper and Row, 1970) quotes both Dean Rusk and Lyndon Johnson as being bitter about the lack of active British assistance in Vietnam (pp. 182–3).

[6] HMSO, Cmnd. 2901.

[7] HMSO, Cmnd. 3357.

[8] *International Herald Tribune* (17 January 1968).

[9] Harold Macmillan, *Hansard*, House of Commons (30 January 1963), col. 956.

[10] For the view that early Anglo-American nuclear relations were not really so close see Andrew J. Pierre, *Nuclear Politics*, p. 25.

[11] See HMSO, *Supply of Ballistic Missiles by the United States to the United Kingdom* (Cmnd. 336, February 1958).

[12] *The Times* (14 April 1960).

[13] Ibid.

[14] L. W. Martin, op. cit., p. 2. Also *The Daily Telegraph* (19 April 1960).

[15] *Hansard*, House of Commons (22 June 1960), col. 396.

[16] Ann Arbor, Michigan (16 June 1962).

[17] See *New York Times* (24 June 1962).

[18] See HMSO, *Polaris Sales Agreement* (Cmnd. 1995, April 1963). An ironical post-script was the revelation that the United States Air Force had successfully fired a Minuteman missile from a C–5A transport on 24 October 1974. See *Air Force Magazine* (January 1975), pp. 28–9.

[19] This point is discussed in Newhouse, *De Gaulle and the Anglo-Saxons*, p. 225.

[20] Henry Kissinger, *The Troubled Partnership* (New York: McGraw-Hill for the Council on Foreign Relations, 1965), p. 14.

[21] Eventually, of course, the MLF idea was dropped by the United States. Kissinger examines this episode in greater detail (ibid.).

[22] M. Camps, *European Unification in the Sixties*, p. 155.

[23] For evidence of this, see the 1964 *Statement on Defence* (Cmnd. 2270), paras 6 and 7.

[24] The Labour government decided not to exercise its option on a fifth.

[25] See HMSO, *Statement on the Defence Estimates 1975* (Cmnd. 5976, March 1975), chapter 1, para. 25.

11 Transactions: Weapons Acquisition

There are three ways for a nation to acquire weapons systems: by national development and production; by purchase from other nations; and by collaboration with other nations in joint development and production.

For Britain, the emphasis in the initial postwar years was on the first method. Three reasons can be seen for this. In the first place, nations, historically, have wanted to be as self-sufficient as possible in matters directly related to national security. Given the uncertainty of alliances, the fear of becoming dependent on another nation for a vital commodity has been a real one. With the increasing complexity and cost of modern weapons, maintaining self-sufficiency has become ever more difficult.

In the second place, the presence of a large and independent weapons sector has been symbolic of world power status. The British have had extensive military commitments in the postwar era and have needed a large arsenal to carry out their obligations. Continuing to produce their own weapons – even when the sophistication and the cost of them had increased tremendously – seemed a natural part of Britain's world role. A striking example of this was the British decision to continue developing nuclear weapons even after the United States had terminated the wartime alliance in this field. In other areas, such as the aircraft industry, the British had long been world leaders.

As a final point, the production of arms has been a profitable business. Selling military weapons to allies, and sometimes to neutrals, is one way to help defray both the high cost of research and development and the balance of payments impact of deploying troops overseas. Additionally, an innovative weapons system may prove a valuable competitor in the world export market. As in the case of the United States, research in the defence field has led to technological 'spinoffs' in non-military items as well. For a nation as sensitive to trade balance as Britain has been, these are important considerations.

The United States and Europe have provided the main alternatives for Britain in finding a new solution to her weapons acquisition problem. Consideration of a new approach goes back several years, although an active change in emphasis did not come until the mid-1960s. An awareness that Britain could not maintain self-sufficiency in sophisticated weapons production was the first necessity. After that, the relative merits of different options were explored in great detail.

On the one hand, Britain's relationship with the United States included extensive arms sales. European countries, meanwhile, were seen as prospective partners for technological collaboration. The necessity to choose at times between these two alternatives has provided an explicit interaction between the two international subsystems. Before considering that aspect, developments within each of the relationships on the weapons acquisition problem need to be examined.

Arms transactions: Britain and the United States

Anglo-American arms sales have received a good deal of attention in recent years. Interest was focused on this sector particularly at the time of both the Polaris sales agreement in 1962 and the British decision in 1967 to purchase F-111s from the United States. In fact, however, this has been a significant area of Anglo-American relations for much of the postwar period.

In terms of both the focus of this study and the actual level of 'importance' involved, attention needs to be centred on British acquisition of American weapons. Three basic patterns are evident, as shown in Table 11.1. Through

Table 11.1

United States military sales to the United Kingdom, 1950–74 ($'000)*

Year	Total
1950–63	58,094
1964	16,118
1965	50,728
1966	66,216
1967	156,856
1968	270,487
1969	369,499
1970	221,535
1971	117,741
1972	79,875
1973	66,198
1974	64,946
1950–74	1538,293

* Deliveries

Source: United States Department of Defense, Security Assistance Agency, *Foreign Military Sales and Military Assistance Facts* (Washington DC, April 1974)

the 1950s, British purchases from the United States were relatively slight. From 1950 to 1963, the total figure was $58 million. In the same period, the United States supplied Britain with over $1 billion of equipment through the Military Assistance Program (MAP).

In the 1960s, after the termination of MAP for Britain, the level of arms purchases rose dramatically. While the Polaris agreement came at the start of this period, the totals are most striking in the later years. Over $1·13 billion of sales were completed between 1967 and 1971.

Finally, since 1971, there has been a decline in British purchases of American arms, although the figures for each year since then are comparable to the total cumulative figures for 1950–63. An understanding of these patterns involves British capabilities, her changing defence policy, and the availability of different weapons sources.

Anglo-American relations have included both military and economic concerns. In the first place, the military establishments of both nations want the best equipment available in order to carry out their function of national defence. With their close security relationship, the United States has not hesitated to make available to Britain her most sophisticated weapons systems. As Table 11.2 shows, the two largest categories for British purchases have been aircraft and missiles.

At the same time, the British have wanted to maintain a weapons production capability of their own. This has been the product partly of traditional national security interests and partly of a global power status. Thus during the 1950s, while Britain was acquiring military assistance from the United States, she was still largely self-sufficient in advanced technology, such as aircraft.

Economic considerations have also been a factor. First, arms exports were, and continue to be, a method of offsetting overseas defence costs as well as offering major opportunities for successful producers. Secondly, export sales may be needed to enable a sufficiently large production run to lower per unit costs to a manageable level. These economic concerns have affected both Britain and the United States, and influenced their military relationship.

On the one hand, there are indications that the British for many years were relatively successful in selling arms to the United States.[1] Both technological advancement and mutual confidence – a pluralistic security community – made such a relationship possible. The first factor has noticeably deteriorated, thus altering sales patterns. While sales of aircraft engines and spacecraft parts continue,[2] the only complete weapons system sold by Britain to the United States in recent years has been the Harrier.

During the same period, the United States has also seen arms sales as one means of defraying defence costs. The use of both promotion and pressure to

Table 11.2a

United States military sales and assistance to the United Kingdom (totals by category): value in $'000

Categories (Including Spares) and Implementing Agencies	Foreign Military Sales (FMS)				Military Assistance Program (MAP)			
	Ordered		Delivered		Programmed		Delivered	
	Cumulative	1974	Cumulative	1974	Cumulative	1974	Cumulative	1974
Total	1971,267	45,079	1525,096	64,946	1034,478	–	1034,478	–
Aircraft	937,560	8,219	842,737	10,037	317,376	–	317,376	–
Ships	5,898	605	3,824	566	2,597	–	2,597	–
Vehicles and weapons	26,389	1,281	22,925	142	115,761	–	115,761	–
Ammunition	86,014	255	32,889	2,905	38,586	–	38,586	–
Missiles	543,609	6,501	392,831	14,550	278,521	–	278,521	–
Communications equipment	27,520	590	25,667	655	150,668	–	150,668	–
Other equipment	34,554	2,464	24,751	11,607	6,778	–	6,778	–
Construction	253	–	253	–	–	–	–	–
Repair and rehabilitation	9,585	3,134	5,966	535	32,381	–	32,381	–
Supply operations	49,471	1,950	34,281	3,049	60,925	–	60,925	–
Training	4,226	70	4,037	76	21,623	–	21,623	–
Other services	193,115	19,957	134,930	20,820	9,262	–	9,262	–
Unspecified and adjustments	53,073	53	–	–	–	–	–	–
Army	218,937	22,832	121,795	21,612	196,830	–	196,830	–
Navy	1399,054	13,362	1089,259	26,596	122,636	–	122,636	–
Air Force	353,277	8,885	314,042	16,738	715,012	–	715,012	–
Other agencies	–	–	–	–	–	–	–	–

Table 11.2b

Quantity of selected items

Selected items	FMS				MAP			
	Ordered		Delivered		Programmed		Delivered	
	Cum.	1974	Cum.	1974	Cum.	1974	Cum.	1974
Aircraft:								
Bomber B-29	–	–	–	–	87	–	87	–
Cargo C-130	66	–	66	–	–	–	–	–
Fighter F-4K	52	–	52	–	–	–	–	–
Fighter F-4M	118	–	118	–	–	–	–	–
Fighter F-86	–	–	–	–	70	–	70	–
Helicopter OH-13	6	–	6	–	–	–	–	–
Helicopter CH-19	–	–	–	–	10	–	10	–
Helicopter UH-19	–	–	–	–	15	–	15	–
Helicopter OH-23	–	–	–	–	20	–	20	–
Patrol P-2	–	–	–	–	52	–	52	–
Miscellaneous	–	–	–	–	707	–	707	–
Ships and craft:								
Fuel oil barge	–	–	–	–	1	–	1	–
Miscellaneous	2	–	2	–	–	–	–	–
Guided Missiles:								
Bullpup	841	–	841	–	–	–	–	–
Corporal	–	–	–	–	113	–	113	–
Polaris	102	–	102	–	–	–	–	–
Sidewinder	1777	–	1777	–	–	–	–	–
Sparrow	1912	–	1912	422	–	–	–	–
Thor	–	–	–	–	72	–	72	–
Miscellaneous	9	–	9	–	–	–	–	–
Combat vehicles:								
Tank recovery	22	–	22	–	–	–	–	–
Miscellaneous combat	–	–	–	–	1334	–	1334	–
Artillery:								
Gun, 175mm SP	46	–	38	–	–	–	–	–
Gun, 175mm towed	24	–	24	–	–	–	–	–
How., 105mm towed	2	–	2	–	–	–	–	–
How., 155mm SP	65	–	50	–	–	–	–	–
How., 155mm towed	2	–	2	–	–	–	–	–
How., 8 inch SP	16	–	16	–	–	–	–	–

Source: United States Department of Defense, Security Assistance Agency, *The Journal* (Washington DC, 1974)

sell American arms has been frequent. In the light of this, the fact that greater pressure to purchase American arms was not exerted on the British might be taken as another measure of a special relationship between them. In this way, and through the Military Assistance Program, the United States helped to subsidise the British world role. As that role changed, and as economic pressures on the United States increased, the weapons relationship in the Anglo-American subsystem also changed.

An example which demonstrates the complexity of the interaction patterns was the sale of F-111s to the UK. The elaborate arrangements made in 1967 to open up American markets to Britain as a means of offsetting the cost of purchasing the F-111 illustrate special concessions, but they also demonstrate the potential for conflict when the presumption of special ties is disappointed.

The process of finding items on which Britain could bid as well as British arms that might be bought by the United States was described by Secretary of Defense Robert McNamara in a Congressional hearing as 'tortuous'.[3] And then, when negotiations were going badly enough anyway, the United States Congress passed the Byrnes Amendment of 1968, which forbade the Navy to purchase from non-American sources.[4] This action had a direct impact on United Kingdom shipyards, which had already won some contracts. The British Defence Minister, Denis Healey, issued a statement warning that the whole relationship between Britain and America might be undermined if any threat to the Anglo-American offset costs agreements developed as the result of the Congress's action.[5] Washington officials reacted to this, promising that means would be found to honour the obligations. The finale to this exercise in Anglo-American harmony came in January 1968, when the British cancelled the F-111 contract after devaluation.

This case is striking, but not entirely atypical. The Buy American Act, under which a low foreign bid on a contract may be rejected when national security is found to favour buying from United States producers, has been a long-standing problem for the British. First of all, they do not think of themselves as just any foreign nation and emphasise the close security arrangements which they have with the United States. Secondly, the British economy sorely needs the trade involved. As the F-111 offset case illustrates, such restrictions have become more of an irritant in the last few years as the United Kingdom tried to increase her arms sales to help balance the rising cost of defence.

Overall, the sales figures would suggest that, prior to the mid-1960s, the primary 'importance' of Anglo-American arms sales was military rather than economic: that is, Britain was supplementing her own production by purchases from the United States. In turn, by 1965 growing economic constraints forced the British to rethink their policy on weapons acquisitions. One of the

114

first actions of the Labour government in 1964 was the appointment of a committee to investigate the state of the aircraft industry. The results, the 1965 Plowden Report,[6] dictated major changes. The relatively small scale of the British home market was making it increasingly difficult to bear the initial costs of developing and producing aircraft (see Table 11.3, the number of new aircraft delivered annually to the UK, as an illustration of this). Among the recommendations for the future were wholehearted collaboration with European countries (discussed below) and increased purchases from the United States when circumstances warranted.[7]

The dramatic increase of arms purchases by the United Kingdom starting in 1966 was concentrated in the area of military aircraft. This policy resulted from the Plowden Report's contention that Britain could reduce her overall defence expenditure by purchasing aircraft from the United States. The immediate implementation of this resulted in the decision to cancel the TSR2 and to purchase the F-111 instead. The economic motive seems to have been foremost. Indeed, some British officials have argued that there was nothing wrong with the TSR2 other than that the British could not afford to develop it.[8]

The two tables of arms purchases – 11.1 and 11.2 – are useful indicators of Britain's changed military fortunes. The independence she once aspired to has

Table 11.3

New aircraft delivered
to the United Kingdom, 1958–73

Year	Number
1958	826
1959	723
1960	518
1961	395
1962	487
1963	450
1964	319
1965	415
1966	431
1967	312
1968	278
1969	500
1970	352
1971	380
1972	246
1973	293

Source: HMSO, Central Statistical Office, *Annual Abstract of Statistics* for the years in question

become too costly. In this sense, she has become more like the United States' other allies, depending heavily on American defence equipment. The United States has always been willing to sell equipment to Britain, but for the British, the financial aspects of these arrangements have become more important since the mid-1960s. No longer is the value of the arms flow predominantly a military one; rather, Britain is emphasising the best price for her military equipment. Therefore the evaluation of alternative weapons sources has become a significant aspect of defence policy.

Technological collaboration: Britain and Europe

The idea of collaboration on advanced and costly weapons systems is not a new one. The Western European Union has made many proposals for an arms pool.[9] Moreover, the British government has declared collaboration to be official policy for a number of years. However, serious consideration of the possibliities is a more recent devlopment. The most striking efforts have been made in the aircraft industry and the following discussion will therefore rely mainly on that field for examples.

The 1958 Defence White Paper noted that discussions were being held with France, Germany and the Netherlands on joint research and development.[10] The 1960 Statement went considerably further, expressing a commitment to the principle of international cooperation in this area:

> If we are to maintain the efficiency of our defensive alliances at a bearable cost, then we must make the best use of the scientific and industrial resources of the free world. It is the Government's wish to promote a wider measure of cooperation in defence research development and production. This involves working as closely as possible with the Commonwealth and the United States of America and with NATO and the Western European Union.[11]

Yet a list, published shortly before this statement, of international agreements for cooperation in scientific research to which the United Kingdom was a party included no examples of weapons collaboration.[12]

The government repeated its commitment to interdependence in 1961, arguing that 'a narrow, nationalist policy for the choice and production of arms makes no sense to-day.'[13] A *Financial Times* report on the aircraft industry later that year estimated that British aircraft, engine and ancillary manufacturers had nearly fifty links of one kind or another with companies on the continent.[14] Some were financial, but most were agreements to sell each other's products or to manufacture them under licence. Possibilities for collaboration were mentioned, but the main emphasis was upon the opportunities for new markets in Europe for the British aircraft industry.

A breakthrough came in 1962. The British and the Dutch agreed on the joint development of the Sea Dart ship-defence missile system. Then, in November of that year, the British and the French concluded an agreement on the joint development of a supersonic aircraft, the Concorde. There were no political benefits associated with this arrangement, however, as de Gaulle still vetoed the British Common Market application a month and a half later.

The year 1962 also saw the signing of the convention for the European Launcher Development Organisation (ELDO). Although originally proposed by the British in 1960 as a means of finding a use for the Blue Streak missile, the project was seen by some as a possible step toward wider European collaboration. Formal operations of ELDO began in February 1964.

A major shift in British policy seems to have come in 1965. The then Minister of Aviation, Roy Jenkins, told the House of Commons in February that 'We are at the end of the road so far as exclusively British manufacture of complicated weapons systems for an exclusively British market is concerned.'[15] The Plowden Report in December concluded that 'Britain must turn increasingly to collaboration with other countries as the means of improving the relationship between size of market and development and initial production costs.'[16] Between these two statements, a number of supportive decisions were made.

The TSR2 was cancelled in April and it was subsequently announced that Britain would purchase the F-111 from the United States instead. Additionally, two military aircraft projects were to be started with France. The first was the Jaguar, to be used as a strike aircraft and as a trainer. The agreement on the second, a variable geometry aircraft, called for preliminary studies. Accompanying these complete weapons systems projects were a number of agreements concluded on aircraft engines. These tended to be bilateral, either Anglo-French or Anglo-German, and drew heavily upon the technological leadership of Rolls Royce.

The efforts described thus far represented an upswing in Anglo-European technological collaboration. While final results had not yet been achieved, the idea of technological collaboration was in vogue. Additionally, political benefits were thought to accrue from these efforts. Specifically, a willingness to join other European nations in this field was thought to be a demonstration of Britain's 'European-ness'.

A number of specific concessions were made by the British in this vein. One of the British participants in the Jaguar project, Elliot Avionics, had several disputes with the French until the British government put pressure on the

E

company to desist. Additionally, the British agreed to finance the variable geometry aircraft up to 1976 in order to relieve the strain on the French budget imposed by the 'force de frappe'.[17] Talks went ahead on a joint airbus project involving France, Germany and Britain, agreement on the specifications being reached in 1967. This latter accord was reached despite British unhappiness with the larger model which Germany wanted.

Soon, however, major difficulties arose. One case was the variable geometry aircraft previously mentioned. In January 1967, a preliminary agreement was reached to go ahead the following year with studies in preparation for work on prototypes. An immediate effort was made to bring in the West Germans before the final technical specifications were made. Then, on 29 June 1967, the French suddenly pulled out of the project. The impact of this decision was not lessened by the knowledge that Dassault was going ahead with his own variable goemetry aircraft, the Mirage G, with French government help.[18]

The British also seemed to develop doubts about the value of some of these projects. An agreement on the airbus had been signed by France, West Germany and Britain in July 1967. After expressing reservations about both the size and the costs of the European A300B, the British withdrew from the project in April 1969 and proceeded with the development of their own airbus the BA-311. In turn, they were criticised for competing against a European project.[19]

A similar fate was in store for ELDO. In February 1966, the British issued a memorandum questioning the future value of ELDO, largely on financial grounds. This led to talks in July of that year at which it was decided to continue with the programme, but with Britain's financial contribution reduced from 39 per cent to 27 per cent.[20] Then, in April 1968, the British announced their decision to withdraw from active participation in ELDO by 1971.

Even a change of government in 1970 did not reverse that decision. However, neither did it end the possibility of a European space effort. The impetus for a re-evaluation came from a United States proposal in July 1970 to develop a joint American–European programme after the Apollo series was completed. Serious policy differences (for example the French desire to proceed with development of a new European launcher against strong British opposition, including withdrawal from ELDO) delayed a European response for over two years, but, in December 1972, the basic agreements were concluded to form a European Space Agency, an amalgamation of ELDO and the European Space Research Organisation (ESRO), and to participate with the United States in a space shuttle programme. A formal agreement was signed in September 1974.

Whether major benefits – technological or political – arise from these efforts seems problematical. The United States seems less enthusiastic about the project than she originally was.[21] Moreover, the difficulties which the Europeans have had in agreeing among themselves on even the initial steps do not seem promising. Finally, the idea of developing a European programme while collaborating with the United States involves the very kind of imbalance that has limited the usefulness of NATO as a vehicle for European integration, and, in fact, has led many Europeans to oppose an Atlantic partnership *until* Europe has developed its own identity and strength.

Some new agreements did follow the series of dissolutions. In April 1967, there was an Anglo-French agreement on joint requirements and development of three helicopters. In this case, two of the models were to be built with the French company Aerospatiale as the prime contractor while the third was to be under the direction of the British firm Westlands.

The helicopter 'package deal', while a less ambitious kind of collaboration, did involve the same balancing of responsibility and benefits that marked other projects. A second stage of cooperation on the project was the announcement on 31 May 1973 that the two firms had formed a new company, Heli-Europe Industries, to market helicopters.[22]

The other new project, in the aftermath of the withdrawal of the French from the variable geometry aircraft, was a six-nation consortium to develop and manufacture a multi-role combat aircraft (MRCA). Three nations dropped out, but Britain, West Germany, and Italy agreed to go ahead with the development stage.

The project represents a serious effort to develop a sophisticated modern weapons system, the first major attempt in the West other than by the United States. The cost is high – and still rising – and the nature of the roles intended for MRCA has changed, but the project is clearly the kind of technological enterprise that individual European nations such as Britain are incapable of carrying out by themselves.

The progress of one other collaborative effort, started earlier, warrants comment. Concorde, while a civil project, has broader implications because of the advanced research and development involved. The first prototype was flown in late 1967 with production models due in 1975. The high expectations have not been fulfilled, however.

Economically, the project has been a disaster. Estimated development costs increased six fold in the first ten years (see Table 11.4). Moreover, the market is, at best, shaky. A number of major carriers, including Pan American and Trans World Airlines, have cancelled their options. Hostility from environment groups raised obstacles to landing in the United States. Even as these kinds of difficulties are being resolved, the long-term demand is far from

Table 11.4

Successive cost estimates for Concorde (£ million)

Date	Estimates of total development costs	Estimates of UK share	Actual UK expenditure to date
November 1962	150–70	75–85	–
July 1964	280	140	–
June 1966	500 (including 50 for contingencies)	250 (plus 30 at research and development establishments)	–
January 1969	–	–	155
March 1969	–	–	170
May 1969	730 (no provision for contingencies)	340	–
January 1970	–	–	200
October 1970	825	405	240
April 1971	885	440	280
July 1971			290 (plus 10 in production costs)
December 1971	–	–	320
March 1972	970	480	330

Source: Roger Williams, *European Technology*, p. 118. Reproduced from the 6th Report from the Expenditure Committee, Session 1971–72, *Public Money in the Private Sector*, HC347, p. 29

certain. The cost, moreover, has involved a significant concentration of government research and development funds which were thus not available for other projects (see Table 11.5).

On the political side, Concorde does not seem to have contributed to Anglo-French harmony. On the contrary, there have been indications that, but for the lack of a withdrawal clause in the initial agreement, the British government might have cancelled the project.[23] Certainly Concorde did not get the British into the EEC any quicker. Moreover, it has not sparked the development of a European technological community. The difficulties with Concorde may have made such a step even more remote.[24]

The initial expectations of European technological collaboration have not been fulfilled. In the first place, the political pay-offs that Britain had anticipated were not forthcoming. Indeed, by the 1970s British officials reached the conclusion that each of these projects did not involve a solemn test of Britain's commitment to Europe.[25]

Yet strong arguments for collaboration, in both the military and the economic sense, still exist. Disappointment resulted because the concept of collaboration did not snowball into a full-scale European technological

Table 11.5

UK assistance to the aerospace industry, 1964–74 (£ million)

	1964–65	1965–66	1966–67	1967–68	1968–69	1969–70	1970–71	1971–72	1972–73	1973–74 (provisional)
Concorde:										
Airframe	3·7	9·2	18·2	24·0	31·1	31·0	44·0	46·1	45·4	47·6
Aero-engine (Olympus 593)	2·1	10·0	15·9	20·5	24·6	19·9	20·5	27·0	25·9	20·8
Other airframe projects:										
HS146										1·2
Trident 2E				1·5	0·4					
Trident 3B				0·2	4·1	5·4	4·9	0·9	–	0·1
Trident Autoland					0·1	0·1	–	–	0·1	–
Airbus (initial development)					0·5	0·7				
BAC 111–500				5·3	3·1	0·6				
Jetstream			0·6	0·5	0·1					
Others	3·1	2·1	0·6	1·5						
Other engine projects:										
RB211				0·5	10·2	28·2	15·2	69·0	50·1	16·2
M45H									3·6	1·9
RB207				1·2	0·7		0·1			
RB178			1·0	0·1						
Spey 506/510/511	2·9	0·2		0·2	0·1	0·1				
Spey 555		1·3	0·5	0·8	0·1					
Spey 512							0·3			

(1) The above amounts represent gross expenditure, and do not take account of amounts repaid to the government under the terms of launching aid and other agreements. The amounts shown for the RB211 are net expenditure after deduction of repayments of short term production financing; (2) For Concorde, in addition to the amounts shown above there were total payments during the period in question of £112·9 million for capital expenditure and £48 million for other intra-mural expenditure at Government establishments; (3) Loans totalling £5·05 million were made to Short Bros and Harland Ltd between 1965 and 1968 in respect of the Skyvan aircraft.

Source: United Kingdom, Department of Trade and Industry, *Trade and Industry* (1 August 1974), p. 225. Reprint of Parliamentary Question of Thursday, 25 July 1974

community. This was due in part to the difficulties encountered in the projects undertaken previously. While it is true that each nation's share of the cost of a particular undertaking was less than if that nation had tried to do the project alone, total costs nevertheless rose because of inefficiency. The effort to coordinate separate national requirements and separate defence industries often led to acrimony and ill-will.[26]

The desire of each nation to realise benefits from a particular project commensurate with her own contribution was an almost impossible objective to meet. The Plowden Report, back in 1965, recognised this problem:

> A weakness of past policies has been that Britain has tended to associate at random with all comers on the merits of individual projects. . . . If, instead, a partnership were formed covering a range of projects, civil and military, there would be scope for distributing the work more efficiently.[27]

This objective certainly has not been met. The ever-changing partners and the fact that most projects have been undertaken on a bilateral basis demonstrate how little progress has been made in this respect.

An assessment of why this has been the case involves considerations fundamental to the entire integration process in Europe. The inherent limitations in trying to foster cooperation among separate national units is clearly illustrated in the technological field. Rather than the snowballing or spillover effect predicted by integration theory, the result has been a sort of backwash phenomenon.[28] Progress has been impeded because the mandate for technological collaboration has been necessarily isolated and limited. The logic of interrelationships between sectors has made this an untenable position.[29]

A few examples might clarify this. For one, prior to British entry into the EEC, customs duties still had to be paid on parts for Jaguar or Concorde when they crossed the Channel. In this sense, the gap between Britain and the European Community was not bridged. Instead Britain, as one of the leading participants in such projects, was constantly reminded of a gap. More significant, however, was the impact on future collaboration of a lack of common requirements. The difficulties over a European airbus provide one example of this. The potentially damaging consequences of too much compromise are demonstrated here by the example of the American F-111, intended for use by both the Navy and the Air Force. In fact, the only solution to this problem is the integration of European defence strategies and operational requirements as a whole. Although NATO has contributed to military standardisation, the limitations of intergovernmental efforts in this field seem apparent.

At this stage, most governments have tended to look to technological collaboration for economic reasons. The rising cost of weapons systems and

122

the difficulty of competing with the United States make this imperative. The economic benefits are construed, ultimately, in national terms. This has led to the concentration on short term, individual, *ad hoc* projects.

There is a paradox here for Britain. The technological situation helped motivate the British to seek close ties with Europe. Yet, because of their formal exclusion from the institutions of Europe up until 1971, as well as a reluctance by all the nations concerned to accept the full supranational implications of technological collaboration, success in this field has been limited. While Britain managed to establish some links with the Continent, this approach proved to be neither a doorway to Europe nor a complete solution to her weapons acquisition problem.

Interaction

The potential for positive interaction between the Anglo-American and the Anglo-European subsystems dates from 1965. To Britain, the United States and Europe represented clearly differentiated alternatives for solving the weapons acquisitions problem. America already had an advanced arms industry that was very active in promoting sales abroad. Indeed, other Western European allies, especially the West Germans, had long relied on the United States as a major supplier of their military arsenals. On the other hand, British officials had finally come to the conclusion that technological collaboration with the United States did not have much of a future.

> The immense resources of the United States make it difficult for us to find projects of mutual benefit. . . . The advantages of collaborating with allies whose resources are more comparable to our own *is* obvious.[30]

Neither were Britain's prospects of major arms sales to or from Western Europe particularly good, as there was no competition with the United States as a supplier in terms of scale. Moreover, there was little optimism about being able to sell European-made weapons to the American military. As the Plowden Report observed, 'There is no chance . . . of Britain ever selling a complete military aircraft to the United States, even as a *quid pro quo* for our adoption of an American type.'[31]

This situation would have posed no problems if the British and other Europeans had been willing to rely to a very great extent on the United States for their advanced weapons systems. In this respect, Britain was clearly in the same position as the other Western European nations. However, besides the natural reluctance to be, and remain, dependent on another nation, many in Europe saw the positive benefits of developing an independent technological capability.

The historical record is rather striking in this regard. As Table 11.6 shows, American aircraft have completely dominated the Western market. The cycle seems to have been repeated in the mid-1970s during the search for a new lightweight fighter to replace the F-104 in several NATO countries. With an initial European market of over $2 billion and a potential world market of over $15 billion, competition was intense. The final decision involved a choice between the YF-16, built by General Dynamics, and the French Mirage F-1 M-53. Despite French appeals to 'buy European' the lower cost and high capability of the American-built plane eventually proved decisive.

Table 11.6

Origins of aircraft in service, 1970 (percentages)

Market	Aircraft originating from		
	EEC	UK	US
EEC	15·2	1·4	83·4
UK	–	71·9	28·1
EEC + UK	10·6	22·4	67·0
Europe	12·8	17·3	69·9
US	0·5	1·6	97·9
Western World	3·8	5·7	90·5

Source: Commission of the European Communities, *A Policy of the Community for the Promotion of Industry and Technology in the Aeronautical Sector* (Brussels, July 1972)

Thus, even with the development of a European consciousness, an independent and competitive European industry in advanced technological weapons systems is far from certain.

It can be argued that the United States has contributed to that difficulty by insisting on selling arms to the Europeans.[32] An effort to redress the balance of payments costs of stationing US troops in Europe has led to considerable pressure on NATO allies to purchase American arms. Additionally, both the opportunities for, and the insistence on, buying American arms may have had the effect of stifling European initiatives to develop their own arms industries. Britain has been right in the middle of this dilemma, having, on the one hand, a high demand for sophisticated weapons systems, and possessing, on the other, the capability to make a significant contribution to any European technological effort. It is a classical example of short versus long term considerations.

American weapons systems have been available immediately. The cost of research and development is avoided directly, although obviously American firms will make a profit on any transaction. At the same time, Europe is dependent on the United States. Because of incidents like the cancellation of Skybolt, some Europeans are cautious. While most want to remain in a military alliance with the United States, they would like to feel that they have some control over their own fate.

The long term solution for Europe has been seen in technological collaboration. For all three reasons[33] that Britain had maintained a national arms industry, there has been a desire to do the same on a European basis. The main obstacles can be reduced to two.

First, it is very difficult to plan or act in the long run. Arms are wanted today, or as soon as possible after a particular need is identified. Further evidence of this pressure has been the suspension by the European Community of any tariff on imported aircraft weighing over 15 tons. This has applied principally to aircraft systems from the United States. As an interesting contrast, the United States has maintained a tariff level of approximately 5 per cent. Thus the American aircraft industry has had an added competitive advantage over any European effort. The long lead time for modern weapons systems has exacerbated the pressure on the Europeans in this area.

Meanwhile, the United States also tends to approach this problem on a short run basis. The revenues obtained from arms sales help relieve pressure on the balance of payment situation. Since the United States has no doubts about her own intentions, it is sometimes hard for Washington to understand why the Europeans should feel uneasy. Since costs are so high, it is not possible to maintain the same level of arms purchases from the United States and also develop a European arms industry. This highlights the dilemma of short versus long term considerations.

Secondly, efforts at European technological collaboration have not been going on in a vacuum. The reasons for their limited success are directly related to developments in the political and economic sectors. This was certainly obvious before Britain became a member of the European Community.[34] The willingness in Europe to make a commitment to far-reaching technological collaboration continues to be limited by the rate of progress in economic and political integration.[35]

In the last few years, the nature of Britain's weapons acquisition needs has changed markedly. This, in turn, has led to the assessment of the relative abilities of the United States and of Europe to provide solutions. As Britain's capability for arms self-sufficiency declined, the 'importance' of both these subsystems in this sector increased. However, in the long term, these two alternatives are not entirely compatible.

Both actual and potential benefits have to be considered. For the most part, the British have chosen the European subsystem as their primary long term orientation. However, since European technological collaboration has developed slowly, the immediate ability of the United States to supply arms has remained 'important'. A third alternative, that of doing without, may receive more serious consideration as certain systems (Polaris, for example) approach obsolescence. The perception of Britain's international role and progress in the development of resources to support a role should be the key factors in making this choice.

Notes

[1] Figures on weapons transactions are generally difficult to acquire and vary so much in form that comparisons are obscured. Classification of statistics is one barrier, but the lack of a comprehensive reporting system seems to be more serious. On the question of British sales to the United States, one unpublished report shows that payments made by the US to Britain for defence purchases exceeded the annual reverse flow in every year between 1954 and 1966. While the picture of reciprocal sales and British economic success presented by those figures seems significant, there is a lack of collaborative sources to verify the information.

[2] See figures in US Department of Commerce, *United States Imports for Consumption and General Imports*, FT 246 series.

[3] *The Daily Telegraph* (11 August 1967).

[4] *The Times* (13 September 1967).

[5] *The Guardian* (15 September 1967).

[6] HMSO, *Report of the Committee of Inquiry into The Aircraft Industry* (Cmnd. 2853, December 1965).

[7] Cmnd. 2853, para. 520 and para. 523.

[8] Financial problems, of a different sort, developed with the Harrier as well. Despite the success in exports, by mid-1975 there was a distinct possibility that the Royal Navy would not be able to afford to buy the Harrier. The possibility of eventual US production was even raised (*The Times*, 25 April 1975).

[9] See the discussion in John Calman, *European Cooperation in Defence Technology* (London: Institute for Strategic Studies, 1967).

[10] HMSO, *Report on Defence: Britain's Contribution to Peace and Security* (Cmnd. 363, February 1958), para. 26.

[11] HMSO, *Report on Defence 1960* (Cmnd. 952, February 1960), para. 48.

[12] *Hansard*, House of Commons (26 January 1960), cols. 23–6.

[13] HMSO, *Report on Defence 1961* (Cmnd. 1288, February 1961), para. 23.

[14] *Financial Times* (17 August 1961).

[15] *Hansard,* House of Commons (9 February 1965).

[16] Cmnd. 2853, para. 240.

[17] See Christopher Layton, *European Advanced Technology* (London: Allen and Unwin, 1969), p. 145.

[18] Ibid., pp. 146–7.

[19] See, for example, *The Times* (18 December 1969).

[20] It could be argued that Harold Wilson's ability to get Britain's financial contribution to ELDO reduced encouraged him in 1974 to try the same approach with the European Community budget.

[21] Roger Williams, op. cit., p. 75.

[22] British Information Service, *Survey of Current Affairs* (June 1973), p. 249.

[23] See Roger Williams, op. cit., p. 119.

[24] One study found that the money spent on developing Concorde could have bought controlling interest in all the major US aircraft and component industries. See Christopher Redmon, 'The European Aircraft Industry', *European Community* (December 1974), p. 9.

[25] *The Times,* in arguing against the Channel tunnel, suggested that since British entry into Europe was assured it was no longer necessary to engage in collaborative projects just to make a political gesture (*The Times,* 7 August 1972.)

[26] See Williams, discussion of management problems in multinational collaboration, op. cit., chapter 5.

[27] Cmnd. 2853, para. 261.

[28] See the discussion of 'spill-back' in Leon Lindberg and Stuart Scheingold, *Europe's Would-Be Polity* (Englewood Cliffs: Prentice-Hall, 1970).

[29] For an argument that disputes this position and suggests, instead, that projects and sectors can be 'encapsulated', see Phillippe Schmitter, 'Central American Integration: Spill-over, Spill-around or Encapsulation', *Journal of Common Market Studies,* vol. 9, no. 1 (September, 1970).

[30] HMSO, *Statement on the Defence Estimates 1966,* Part 2 (Cmnd. 2902, February 1966), chapter 6, para. 20.

[31] Cmnd. 2853, para. 247. This assesment was over-pessimistic, as the sale of the Harrier demonstrates.

[32] See, for example, Calman, op. cit., p. 15.

[33] See p. 109.

[34] See *The Economist* (14 October 1967), p. 119.

[35] See Williams, op. cit., p. 150.

PART III

POLITICAL RELATIONS

12 Anglo–European Political Relations

> There is one thing you British will never understand: an idea. And there is one thing you are supremely good at grasping: a hard fact. We will have to build Europe without you – but then you will have to come in on our terms. (Jean Monnet, 1951.)

The most significant indicator of Britain's search for a political role in the years between 1958 and 1975 were her three separate attempts to join the European Community. These efforts reversed a historical British position. Throughout the entire postwar era, Britain was faced with the necessity of coming to terms with developments on the Continent, but her previous attitude can be summed up in Winston Churchill's phrase that Britain was 'with but not of' Europe.[1] Indeed, even after finally achieving membership of the European Community, there was lingering uncertainty in Britain over her political role.

Much of the history and details of British relations with the European Community are described in other portions of this book. Works which examine British negotiations for membership of the Community have also been cited. The focus of this chapter is upon the implications of those actions and events for Britain's search for a political role.

British negotiations with the European Community

The European Community of which Britain became a formal member on 1 January 1973 has changed significantly since 1958. One leading student of international integration wrote in 1967 that 'European integration has slowed since the mid-1950s, and it has stopped or reached a plateau since 1957–58'.[2] This assessment seems unduly gloomy. Certainly the integration process has not advanced as rapidly as its advocates may have wished, but the shape of Europe is undoubtedly different today to what it was in 1958.[3]

Indeed, the first four years of the Common Market saw first, survival, and then, prosperity. The tariff-cutting schedules were accelerated. Talks were held on political union. The United States recognised the impact of the organisation. And the British were sufficiently attracted to apply for membership, thus reversing their policy of opposition and obstruction.

The public posture of British leaders placed the greatest emphasis on the economic reasons for joining the Common Market. It has been argued that this was necessary to satisfy a domestic constituency which was opposed to any submerging of British sovereignty within a supranational grouping, and that, in fact, political considerations were the controlling ones for the British government.[4] Still, it seems clear that the British were unwilling to join a federal Europe in 1961 or to work for its development in the near future. Having decided that an institutional commitment was no longer avoidable, British officials were determined to keep their participation as limited as possible and to maintain maximum freedom of action.

The pattern of negotiations demonstrated several factors. Neither side gave overriding priority to being in the same organisation as the other. The British maintained their belief in their special role in the world, and insisted that appropriate accommodations be made for them. Furthermore, it was felt that other alternatives were available and that the British could choose to join or not to join. On the part of the Community, the addition of Britain was seen as desirable, but not essential. The commitment to the Treaty of Rome definitely came first. It is fair to say that attitudes differed within the Common Market on what terms would be acceptable for British membership, but the desire not to compromise the Community was paramount.

The first application presented a number of dilemmas. It was definitely a turning point in Britain's relations with Western Europe. On the other hand, the commitment which the British were prepared to make was neither as total as some would have liked nor of the kind that others wanted. De Gaulle wanted a United Kingdom which would follow his lead unquestioningly while 'Europeans' in the Community hoped for a British willingness to subscribe to supranationalism. These different conceptions of the Community obviously complicated Britain's task of negotiating membership.

Thus, having finally made the historical decision and undergone a long and often bitter debate about its merits, the British were right back where they started, or even a little worse off. For in making their application, they had lessened the availability of the Commonwealth link, and in having that application rejected, they had made their Atlantic ties more difficult to maintain.

De Gaulle's veto in 1963 led to considerable ill-will, but did not result in the break-up of the Community. This was the first of a series of crises which the Common Market survived. On the other hand, from this period on the momentum of integration slowed, as other nations also employed the veto on issues of national concern.

The second British application involved a very different set of circumstances. In the first place, it was undertaken by a Labour government, recently converted to a European orientation. Secondly, the approach was overtly political,[5] and attempted to respond to the criticisms expressed in de Gaulle's 1963 veto. And, if the immediate result was the same – another veto by de Gaulle – the British reaction was very different from that of 1963. Wilson insisted on maintaining the application and, in fact, attempted to rebut the substance of de Gaulle's objections to British membership of the Community.

Moreover, the application provoked a crisis of sorts within the Community. Although negotiations never began, France's five partners had all expressed an interest in British membership by the time of de Gaulle's refusal. What was significant was their willingness *after* the veto to support Britain's claim. By this time, the integration process within the Common Market seemed to be at a standstill. While loyalty to the Community was maintained, new initiatives were not forthcoming. The shadow of de Gaulle loomed over everyone in Brussels. Even with his departure from office in April 1969, caution was in evidence. A breakthrough did not come until a Community summit conference held at The Hague at the end of 1969. That meeting led to claims of a rebirth of the integration process. With the lead taken by Chancellor Willy Brandt of West Germany, whose country was becoming more assertive in Western Europe, the Community agreed to open negotiations with Britain the following June.

A political event of some importance occured prior to the scheduled opening of negotiations on 30 June 1970. In the British General Election of June, the Labour government was replaced by Edward Heath's Conservative Party. *The Times* noted that the issues remained the same despite the shift in government,[6] but that change was nevertheless significant.

On the one hand, there seemed to be some historical justice in returning Edward Heath to preside over the negotiations, since Heath had been the chief negotiator during the first round of talks which were terminated by de Gaulle's 1963 veto. He was also generally regarded as a committed 'European', in contrast to Harold Wilson's pragmatic conversion to the European cause. It was assumed by some that Heath's well-known support might lessen the difficulty of the bargaining. That expectation was not fulfilled, in the sense that the negotiations were hard-fought, often tedious, and, at times, acrimonious.[7]

Heath, of course, had domestic opinion to keep in mind, as well as the demands of the Community members, particularly France, who were still not willing to limit the discussions to the principle of British membership, leaving the details to be worked out later. Britain's increasing economic woes lessened her bargaining power in the talks, and also made the calculation of the costs and benefits of Community membership more sensitive. Finally, Heath's understanding of the dynamics of the Community process made him see membership as an opportunity, not a sure thing, which required adjustments and a major effort by the British.[8]

At the same time, Heath's political commitment played a part. He certainly saw Britain's future political role within the context of a united Europe.[9] Moreover, the breakthrough in negotiations came after the Heath–Pompidou meeting of 20–21 May 1971.[10] That summit would not have succeeded in the absence of progress in ministerial meetings, but the demonstration of political will was needed for the final step. By contrast, in 1963, the French President had terminated negotiations on which many points had been resolved.

In the long term, however, the fall of Harold Wilson in 1970 may have had a greater impact on Britain's relationship with the Community than did Edward Heath's opportunity to direct the negotiations. Prior to the 1970 election, Wilson was on record in the strongest terms as supporting British membership. Moreover, Wilson had talked continually of the political benefits involved. However, two qualifications need to be mentioned. First, he did not advocate supranationalism. Indeed, his opposition to European federalism even as he supported political unity had a distinctly Gaullist tone.[11] Secondly, Wilson, judged by his actions, seemed to see European development within an Atlantic context. This may have been merely the result of a need to obtain American assistance, particularly economic, but this outlook tended to distinguish Wilson's position from that of Heath even more than the first factor.

In the light of Wilson's record prior to 1970, it is not unreasonable to assume that he would have taken Britain into the Common Market had he remained in office. In opposition, however, his concerns were very different. Much of the Labour Party had always been reluctant about Europe, and Wilson's leverage over them was diminished. Public opinion fluctuated, but large numbers continued to oppose membership. For Wilson, the pragmatist, the pressures to use the Common Market as an electoral issue became overwhelming.

The fact that he attempted to gain public support by opposing the terms of entry negotiated by the Conservatives is neither surprising nor necessarily important. What is significant, however, is that after so many years of discussion, the British remained so divided on the question of EEC membership.

In this sense, even the successful completion of negotiations with the Community did not represent an unequivocal decision on Britain's political future. Where once the choice seemed to be the *direction* of her political role, by the 1970s the issue had shifted to the *kind* of political role Britain would pursue. Economic and military capabilities have affected that choice, but political will and a sense – some have said loss – of identity have also been influential. The record of British membership in the Community clearly illustrates this last point.

Britain in the European Community

With the successful negotiations on enlargement, a general mood of optimism seemed to prevail in Europe for the first time in several years. This optimism was symbolised by the agreements made at the European Summit meeting in Paris in October 1972. At that session, the first at which all the nations of the enlarged Community met, a timetable was adopted for achieving European economic and monetary union by 1980. In addition to expanding Community activity to another economic sector, the step had clear implications for the strengthening of the integration movement as a whole.

These high expectations were totally shattered by the events of 1973, Britain's first year of membership. If Europe had been seen as the focus for a new political role, it became evident that the internal unity needed for world influence was lacking and that the international system was becoming more pluralistic and less stable. By the end of the year, the prospects for maintaining the schedule toward economic and monetary union already seemed diminished. An emphasis on separate national interests was more apparent than ever.

Two developments – both more than single events – highlighted Europe's political malaise. The first involved the long-standing issue of determining Europe's relationship with the United States. In April, Henry Kissinger, the American Secretary of State proposed a new Atlantic Charter as a device for promoting closer relations within the Atlantic area. The European nations, while responding individually to Kissinger's ideas, had considerable difficulty in formulating a joint position. Even the formal statement that was agreed upon in September did not produce a greater sense of European cohesion or an Atlantic dialogue.

Subsequent to the Copenhagen Summit in December, the Nine issued a 'Declaration on Europe's Identity', which, among other things, spoke of a constructive dialogue with the US 'on the basis of equality and in the spirit of friendship'.[12] A later Community document, assessing the effects of membership on Britain, chided the British by observing that 'Had Britain not been a member of the Community, she could never have hoped to cooperate with the USA "on the basis of equality".'[13] At this point in time, however, neither has the Community as a whole.

The Copenhagen Summit was also noteworthy for displaying European political disarray in the face of a new international political force, Arab oil interests. The Middle East War in October had led to an oil embargo which hit Europe particularly hard. Despite numerous Community policy statements on energy in previous years, the response of European nations to the oil crisis and to accompanying Arab political pressure was fragmented and individualistic. The split within the Community became even wider and more visible in Washington in February 1974 when France broke with her Common Market partners in an effort to negotiate a joint bargaining position among the oil-importing nations.

The period after the Washington conference did not produce a substantial reduction in the fragmentation of the Community. On the other hand, neither did the Community structure completely come apart as some predicted it would. Perhaps it was fortunate that attention had to be focused on an 'internal' issue, the British renegotiation of membership terms. The political crises of 1973 and 1974 strongly suggest that an adequate level of cohesion is still lacking for the Community to play an influential or effective political role in the world.

In the period since then efforts have concentrated on improving the consultative mechanism within the Community. The Paris Summit of December 1974 produced a decision to hold meetings of the Council of the Communities three times a year, or as needed. This movement toward frequent summitry does provide a forum for political discussion, although it also moves the initiative away from the Community institutions back to the member nations.

Whether this arrangement enables the Nine to better deal with international crises or to formulate unified positions remains to be seen. With the British referendum concluded, other issues of Community building will be pushed forward. The extent of British commitment will be one factor in the success of these efforts, but it is not likely to be decisive. The Community's political impact continues to be limited by the preference for national decision-making.

In broad terms, there are three different possibilities for Europe's future. None are pre-determined; all are a matter of choice. One is disintegration and a breakdown of those agreements which have already been made. Negative 'spillover', a failure to maintain the momentum of the integration process, continuing national differences and disputes – these could lead to a termination of the integration movement and a return to the Europe of individual nations of the past. In the light of the costly history of national competition in Europe, of the formidable machinery created since the Second World War, and of the specific gains already achieved by the European Community, the process of disintegration would certainly be resisted. It would occur no more automatically than has the process of integration. However, because the costs would, for the most part, be apparent and high, this does not seem a likely development.

A far greater possibility is for the continuation of different kinds of functional cooperation without the attainment of a political community. There have been very real gains to individual nations from the economic arrangements which have been made. These could be continued, perhaps with additional agreements concluded on specific areas as the need was felt. While there would be a constant state of tension between those who wanted to limit cooperation and those who sought political integration, such a situation would not necessarily be unstable. This arrangement might evolve into a political confederation with a significant measure of economic integration.

Finally, the possibility of achieving political union in Europe still exists. Perhaps the setbacks are only temporary and the process just needs more time and effort. Indeed, perhaps an experience such as the discord caused by the energy crisis will ultimately contribute to political integration by underscoring the weakness and vulnerability of the nation state. Perhaps. But at this point in time, such a result is neither inevitable nor highly likely.

These developments have, in turn, affected British actions and attitudes. By early 1974, the Community was not fulfilling the hopes of those who saw Britain's political role within an active influential Europe. Moreover, there was, as one Community commentator put it, a 'Eurogloom' in Britain about the initial economic impact of membership.[14] Public opinion polls showed a marked increase in those who thought Britain had made a mistake in joining the Common Market.[15] And, whether there was any connection between this and membership or not, all dimensions of Britain's economy worsened in 1973 and 1974.

Against this background, the opposition Labour Party called for re-negotiation of the terms of entry. Harold Wilson shed his former commitment to Europe, because his party was badly split on the issue and because it appeared that the public was also. The sharp deterioration of economic conditions and a costly and acrimonious strike by coal miners led Edward Heath to call a General Election in February 1974.[16] While Common Market membership was not directly the major campaign issue, the Labour Party's Election Manifesto did promise a renegotiation of terms with the results to be put to a referendum. The Labour victory – actually a minority government – and a second narrow triumph in October led to a formal reopening of the issue of British membership in the European Community.

Between April 1974, when Foreign Secretary James Callaghan, in a speech to the Council of Ministers, outlined the matters which the British wanted to discuss, and June 1975, when the British referendum was held, the process of renegotiation dominated the attention of the Community as well as the political debate in Britain on her role.

The Government White Paper of March 1975, reporting the results of the renegotiations, concluded that Community membership was of 'fundamental importance for Britain's place and role in the world.'[17] The anti-Marketeers, in addition to discussing 'price of butter' issues, made much of the threat of a loss of sovereignty within the Common Market during the referendum campaign. It would be hard to prove, however, that this was the decisive issue in the referendum. Whether the 'yes' vote was a positive political choice, a mere avoidance of greater uncertainty, or just the product of a well-organised campaign, will best be shown by Britain's future performance in the European Community.

To pursue this point returns us to perceptions of the *kind* of role Britain can play, and to the matter of national will. If numerous commentators have remarked on the political disunity of the European Community, such observations have been even more prevalent with respect to Britain. Analysis and introspection, sometimes accompanied by prophecies of disaster, have been rampant. In the 1960s, these kinds of discussions centred on the direction of Britain's role, as in Dean Acheson's 1962 remarks. In the 1970s, the examination has turned more inward, to the kind of nation Britain is, or wants to be.[18] These analyses either argue that the British no longer desire to play any significant political role, or, more ominously, that British society itself is coming apart. Neither contention is totally implausible and the two are somewhat related. Internal instability would seemingly preclude a political role. Domestic uncertainty has undoubtedly contributed to the difficulties of the past. There is, moreover, no firm assurance that the future will be different. Yet, if Britain is to play any significant political role, the future must be different.

The results of the referendum on Common Market membership are seen by some as a positive indicator.[19] A real test will take some time, of course, but the vote should serve the purpose of ending the national debate about Common Market membership. Whether it translates itself into 'unity in tackling the country's economic problems',[20] as Harold Wilson remarked the next day, will be the more important result. The link between economic success and a political role is clear. For Britain to have either, she may need both.

If Britain is to have a political role, it will be in Europe. Whether she does, though, depends on developments in the international system and in the European Community as well as in Britain. The implicit assumption of Dean Acheson's comments in 1962 was that finding a role was a matter of choice for Britain. Even if that were true then, events have demonstrated that the task is far more complex today, and the result far less certain.

Notes

1 In a speech to the House of Commons, 11 May 1953.

2 Karl Deutsch et al., *France, Germany, and the Western Alliance* (New York: Charles Scribner, 1967), p. 218.

3 For a more optimistic assessment of the progress, see Ronald Inglehart, 'An End to European Integration?', *American Political Science Review*, vol. 12, no. 1 (March 1967).

4 See, for example, M. Camps, *Britain and the European Community*, p. 274.

5 See, for example, George Brown's statement of the British position in July 1967. HMSO, *Membership of the European Communities: A Statement Made on Behalf of Her Majesty's Government by the Secretary of State for Foreign Affairs at the Meeting of the Council of the Western European Union at The Hague on 4 July 1967* (Cmnd. 3345, July 1967).

6 Peter Strafford, 'The Six and Britain: Issues Behind Next Week's Talks,' *The Times* (24 June 1970).

7 For a fuller account see Uwe Kitzinger, *Diplomacy and Persuasion*.

8 See, for example, HMSO, *The United Kingdom and the European Communities* (Cmnd. 4715, July 1971). This document was Heath's report on the outcome of negotiations and his recommendation to join the Community.

9 Ibid., paras 26–39.

10 *New York Times* (22 May 1971).

11 See, for example, *The Times* (21 January 1970).

12 European Community Information Service, 'Communiqué of European "Summit" Meeting and Annexes', *Background Note*, no. 29-1973 (20 December 1973), p. 13.

13 European Parliament, *The Effects, in 1973, on the United Kingdom of Membership of the European Community* (July 1974), chapter 1, p. 3.

14 Martin Mauthner, 'Britain's Second Thoughts', *European Community* (December 1973), p. 20.

15 'Gallup Records British Discontent with Community', *European Community News* (17 May 1974).

16 For a discussion of both the General Elections of 1974 see Howard R. Penniman (ed.), *Britain at the Polls: The Parliamentary Election of 1974* (Washington, DC: American Enterprise Institute for Public Policy Research, 1974 and 1975).

17 *European Community* (25 April 1975), p. 11.

18 A sampling of this kind of analysis would include 'The Prospects of Britain', *The Times* series of editorials in the spring of 1971; Norman Macrae's special supplement for *The Economist*, 'The People We Have Become' (28 April 1973); and a steady stream of articles by foreign observers. For three

American examples, see Thomas R. Guthrie, 'Behind The Mask, An Uptight Little Island' (*Cleveland Plain Dealer*, 1 October 1974); Joseph Alsop, 'Great Britain's Loss of National Will' (*Washington Post*, 16 October 1974); and Gwynne Dyer, 'Britannia Is Slipping Under Waves She Once Ruled' (*Washington Star*, 18 May 1975).

[19] Roy Jenkins called it '. . . D-Day for a British resurgence' (*The Times*, 7 June 1975).

[20] Ibid.

13 Anglo–American Political Relations: Special and Ordinary

In 1958, British leaders saw a 'special relationship' with the United States as the basis for the UK's political role in the world. While the pattern of relations was disrupted by the Suez crisis, subsequent efforts to strengthen the bond between Britain and America met with a considerable measure of success. A number of factors contributed to this, and it should be stressed that the process of coalition building was a very conscious one; that is, both nations were aware of an alliance between them and were, moreover, cognisant of both its benefits and its costs. This consciousness is significant for a number of reasons.

First, a calculation of benefits and costs suggests a coalition can be dissolved as well as strengthened, depending on changes in the needs and capabilities of its members.[1] To be sure, the cost-benefit analysis has probably not been very precise. Thus the latitude for bargaining within the coalition is increased. Nevertheless, reassessment of the value of a particular alignment is always a possibility.

Secondly, only if the alliance is seen as a conscious process can the background conditions be put into perspective. Because there are so many favourable conditions, some have seen the 'special relationship' as the result solely of background. In this vein, George Ball wrote that the 'special relationship is more the product of sociological affinity than of political agreement.'[2] Such an analysis, however, makes it extremely difficult to understand changes in the pattern of this relationship.

Background conditions are undoubtedly significant. In the first place, they were important in the formation of an Anglo-American alliance. Secondly, their existence also increases the flexibility of bargaining between the two nations. Finally, that 'sociological affinity' reduces the likelihood of a total dissolution of this subsystem. On the other hand, background conditions are not absolute political determinants. Rather, as the history of Anglo-American relations shows, changing needs, capabilities, and interests affect and alter the nature of the alignment.

Background conditions

The United States and Britain share a common language, culture, and legal tradition. In addition, at least throughout this century, the habits of co-operation and the attitude of alliance have been fostered. These reached extraordinary dimensions during the Second World War, and their emotional residue is still evident.

The British and the Americans have felt greatly at ease working together, perhaps because there is no need for translators, perhaps because both approached problems from a similar perspective. Contacts have been built up on all levels and with an air of informality that is absent in most diplomatic relations. A testimony to this atmosphere was offered by Dean Rusk: 'We can't break with Britain. We have to be able to discuss world problems with someone. We can't discuss them with de Gaulle. . . . We and the British don't always agree. But we discuss.'[3]

Such contacts have not always led to accord or even to understanding. In some instances, things may be left unsaid because it is assumed that the other side is thinking on the same wavelength. The channels of communication between London and Washington are almost too numerous at times.[4] The closeness of the alliance does not ensure sensitivity to domestic and bureaucratic pressure.[5]

One source of difficulty has been the imbalance of the alliance. Throughout the postwar period the United States has clearly been the dominant partner. Thus the imbalance is not new. Still, the alliance has been, at times, 'important' to both partners. From the perspective of alliance theory, then, an unfavourable background condition was, for many years, overcome.

Although neither the United States nor Britain has repudiated its Anglo-Saxon background, the 'special relationship' has clearly changed in nature. One American diplomat described the 'special relationship' as the function of a power relationship which no longer exists. According to another, fifteen years ago the United States would not have made any major moves without telling Britain. This is clearly no longer the case.[6]

A historical examination of the pattern of Anglo-American political relations since 1958 demonstrates how the 'special relationship' has fitted into Britain's search for a role. First, it may be asked if the alliance with the United States provided a viable political role in itself. Secondly, what impact did the link with America have on the United Kingdom's consideration of other alignments?

The special relationship as a political role

There have been no formal negotiations between the United States and Britain on the maintenance of a 'special relationship'. Moreover, there are no absolute indicators of the condition of the alliance because it lacks a precise definition. Indeed, the 'special relationship' has been buried and resurrected repeatedly by both politicians and the press.

Emphasis has to be placed on psychological and on subjective factors in making an analysis. The British have constantly had to assess whether the political relationship with the United States meets their need for a political role. Moreover, they have also had to assess the appearance to others of the Anglo-American alliance. Thus, as Henry Kissinger noted in 1965, 'Whatever the "reality" of the "special relationship", Britain has tried to give the impression to the outside world that American policy is strongly influenced, if not guided, by London.'[7]

For these various reasons, it is not always possible to separate form from substance in Anglo-American political relations. Moreover, the substance included contacts and consultation which did not always have visible output. Therefore, in concentrating on the public arena, historical instances are significant in either augmenting or detracting from the *appearance* of a 'special relationship'.

Despite the Suez crisis of 1956, close political relations seem to have been firmly re-established by 1958. The clearest manifestation of this was in the area of nuclear cooperation.[8] In addition, however, the close personal relationship between Macmillan and Eisenhower received considerable attention. A *Christian Science Monitor* article concluded that

> Top-level contacts between the two English-speaking nations already are very good . . . restoration began at Suez. . . . What is new, however, is the depth of cooperation that now is developing. It is being encouraged by both sides at lower echelons as well as at the top.[9]

Each of the main elements, the nuclear and the personal, continued over the next two years as evidence of special Anglo-American relations. In the case of the former, 1960 saw the United States offer Britain her most sophisticated missile system, Skybolt. At least in appearance, this move strengthened the relationship at the time.

The personal side also received much emphasis. In December 1959, Western leaders met in Paris. Partly through the initiative of Harold Macmillan, an East–West summit was scheduled for the next year. This was seen by the British as an opportunity to exercise political influence at the global level.

The cancellation of that meeting after the U-2 incident therefore represented a setback for British political hopes.

Then the 1960 American presidential election was seen as damaging to the British political role. The British felt that President Kennedy and his advisers would not maintain the emotional attachment to the link with the United Kingdom held by President Eisenhower. Indeed, a widely-circulated story about Macmillan's first meeting with Kennedy in April 1961, recounts that Macmillan asked the new President how he felt about the 'special relationship', to which Kennedy allegedly replied, 'What "special relationship"?' Although probably apocryphal, this account is revealing of how precarious the link was felt to be. In fact, Macmillan and Kennedy got along well and the personal side of the 'special relationship' remained quite strong during the next three years.

Notwithstanding that fact, the autumn and winter of 1962 saw serious difficulties. Britain was informed only routinely about American moves in the Cuban missile crisis. Moreover, in the aftermath of Cuba, Britain and the United States had their own missile crisis over the cancellation of Skybolt.

Only two years before, the British had abandoned a totally independent deterrent and chose to rely on the development of the American airborne missile, Skybolt. Secretary of Defense Robert McNamara, unhappy over both the rising costs and the continued technical difficulties of the missile, decided that the project had to be cancelled. The process of communicating the decision to the British and getting their reactions to it demonstrated the problems that even close allies can have in making themselves understood. Both London and Washington waited for the other to make the next move – an offer of a substitute or a request for a replacement. The British were not directly consulted on the original decision and the sensitivity of the step for them was not fully appreciated. Similarly, British officials made an insufficient effort to transmit their views to Washington.

The potential for crisis built up on two levels: misunderstanding, and eventually bitterness in private; and a growing public dispute. The issue of the nuclear deterrent – both its existence and its form – was of major political importance in the United Kingdom. What seemed to some as high-handed American behaviour posed a potential threat not only to ties with Britain, but also to confidence in the United States by her other allies. By early December, a major conflict was brewing.

The routine semi-annual meeting between Kennedy and Macmillan at Nassau in mid-December developed into one of major importance. Henry Brandon described the mood of the British delegation at the conference as 'a resentment and suspicion of American intentions such as I have never experienced in all the Anglo-American conferences I have covered over the last twenty years.'[10] However, the outcome of this ominous beginning was the American offer to the British of the Polaris missile and a confirmation to many that the 'special relationship' was still in force.

What Nassau demonstrated was that a purely technical decision could not override the 'special relationship'. Even before he arrived at Nassau, Kennedy had agreed to let Britain continue with the Skybolt project, with the United States paying 50 per cent of the development costs. At Nassau, Macmillan rejected this compromise. He contended that the value of Skybolt had been gravely depreciated by the American rejection of it. From there, Macmillan argued that the United Kingdom had to have a replacement to maintain the commitment made by the United States at the time of Skybolt in 1960. This plea was set in the context of maintaining the Anglo-American alliance.[11] This premise was accepted by President Kennedy who was unwilling to cast aside what was left of the 'special relationship'.[12]

That a decision had been reached to make available to Britain America's most advanced missile system showed a close security relationship within the subsystem. That the decision was made in two days showed an ability to work together and confidence in overall agreement on objectives. That the decision was contrary to what was expected before the conference began demonstrated that the 'special relationship' was unpredictable. The agreement represented a high point in cooperation, but the circumstances showed that underlying difficulties did exist. The aftermath of the Nassau conference led to a highlighting of those problems.

As an affirmation of close Anglo-American ties, the Polaris agreement was short-lived. In the first place, the bitter feelings which had preceded Nassau were not entirely placated. The British were shown to be clearly dependent on the United States for nuclear capability. Secondly, while the possibility that the Polaris deal might hinder Britain's negotiations with the Common Market was recognised at Nassau and afterwards, the British did not disclaim the alliance with the United States after de Gaulle's veto.[13] It is going too far to say that Macmillan chose between the United States and Europe at Nassau – he had hoped for both. Yet, if a choice had to be made, the British indicated by their actions that the link with the United States still had first priority as the basis of a political role.

For Washington, with the idea of a Grand Design shattered by de Gaulle's veto, the alliance with Britain was to deteriorate in value. The burst of enthusiasm for Atlantic partnership in the early 1960s was sparked by the British Common Market application. A role for her close ally was seen in bridging a gap between America and Europe and also in providing the stability which the emerging Community needed. For their part, the British saw leadership as practically synonymous with membership. Yet after 14

January 1963 none of this was possible. The Grand Design may well have been a last effort to give meaning to the 'special relationship'. Afterwards, the form remained without the substance.

Britain's ability to contribute to an alliance with the United States decreased. That she continued to need the assistance of the United States was evident, but hardly 'special'. Still, the decline was gradual rather than abrupt.

The British reluctance about the MLF proposal has already been discussed. Of course, Anglo-American disagreements were nothing new. The possibility of a Labour government in 1964 was seen by some as a prelude to a further deterioration of relations within the subsystem, considering Labour's position against the nuclear deterrent. Yet once in office, the Labour Party emphasised all the policies which were important to the tie with America. Harold Wilson supported a presence East of Suez, although for different reasons than the Conservatives. The British did not dispose of the nuclear deterrent, but reaffirmed their commitment to NATO. And when Labour realised the dimensions of the economic crisis which they had inherited, the immediate reaction was to go to Washington for help. Despite the opposition of the left wing of the Labour Party, Wilson was to continue this course of action.

Meanwhile, a crucial issue was building up in South East Asia. From 1965 onwards, as the United States became increasingly more committed in the Vietnam war, she found a lack of support from her allies in Western Europe, to say nothing of a lack of material assistance. The Wilson government, again despite considerable opposition within the Labour Party, was the only major ally to give vocal support to the American effort. Even as late as 1970, foreign policy spokesmen for the United Kingdom were reiterating this support.[14]

During the second Common Market application, Lord Chalfont officially disavowed any British claims to a 'special relationship' with the United States.[15] Yet in other speeches, and in actions, the British occasionally hesitated to do so.[16] The problem was not always so much the explicit relationship with the United States as a world outlook which tended to be associated with America. Although they were aware of the conflicts involved, the struggle to reorient their thinking about a political role was not easy for the British. *The Economist*, a long-time advocate of Common Market membership, summed up the dilemma thus:

> For most of this century it has been natural for Englishmen to think of themselves as part of the English-speaking world, of which the United States has become the visible leader. Only now are they beginning in any number to think of themselves as Europeans as well.[17]

Long-standing habits and contacts had obscured the real change in the substance of the 'special relationship' in the mid-1960s. Thus there continued

146

to be arguments about the vitality of the alliance in those years. Yet three events in 1967 demonstrated quite clearly that the 'special relationship' was played out.

In July of that year, the initial decision on phased withdrawal of British troops East of Suez was announced. This step was the first in ending Britain's global presence, and a major area of visible partnership with the United States was thus eliminated. In November, the pound sterling was devalued. That move and the austerity measures which followed underscored the extent of British economic weakness. Finally, the British application to the European Community in 1967, a decision that was not predicated upon the expectation of Atlantic partnership, signalled a realisation by the British that there was no political role left in the 'special relationship'.

The pattern of political relations in the Anglo-American subsystem remained fairly constant after 1967. The numerous contacts ensured that the two nations continued to assign some 'importance' to the relationship. Still, in the political sector, the label 'special' was definitely out of date.

Anglo-American relations since the late 1960s have been basically subsumed within the broader context of European-American relations, in which there has been a general deterioration. The broad outlines of that pattern can be traced, as can indicators of a lingering distinction – whether real or illusory – in Anglo-American relations.[18]

An understanding of the growing divergence in policy interest is essential. First, Britain increasingly focused on Europe and on her economic plight. In contrast, the United States, despite domestic dissent, maintained a global orientation, although she also had economic concerns of her own. Habits of cooperation, common language, and sociological affinity were consistently pre-empted by differing goals. The New York Times, which had helped perpetuate the discussions about a 'special relationship', summarised clearly the changes that had occurred at the time of a Heath–Nixon summit in late 1971:

> An old alliance is like an old marriage; it has to be worked at. But the useful work President Nixon and Prime Minister Heath did at Bermuda to repair the Anglo-American alliance, damaged by six months of unilaterial American economic and diplomatic action, will not restore the partnership of the past. For in the interim, the context in which future relations between the United States and Britain must evolve has been profoundly altered by two events: London's decision to enter the Common Market and Mr Nixon's August 15 announcement of a new foreign economic policy.[19]

In fact, domestic economic concerns and differing world orientations reinforced each other as causes of conflict across the Atlantic. Four developments – overlapping and interrelated – in the 1970s illustrate the relationship directly. The first was President Nixon's new economic policy, announced on 15 August 1971, which included a 10 per cent surcharge on imports and a refusal to convert dollars into gold. The policy was seen by European nations as a threat to international economic relations which required a common stand. Over the next few months, criticism and discussions followed, leading in December to a new formal effort at cooperation, the Smithsonian Agreement.

Even that agreement – so lavishly praised by President Nixon – was marked by a continuing divergence in European and American interests. While Secretary of State Rogers was asserting that the United States continued to support European unity,[20] Secretary of Treasury John Connally was pressuring European ministers to increase their defence commitments in exchange for American economic cooperation. Certainly, the effort was heavy-handed and increased European resentment, but Connally's actions reflected, rather than caused, the split in European-American relations.

An apparent effort to heal the rift came with Secretary of State Henry Kissinger's call for a new Atlantic Charter in a speech in April 1973.[21] The speech was billed as the springboard for a 'year of Europe' in American foreign policy, but the results were negligible.

Kissinger, while reasserting the US commitment to Europe and implying that Atlantic relations would receive more attention, continued to link monetary, trade, and defence issues as John Connally had. The immediate European response was favourable to the broad idea, but negative about the linking of issues. The British comments were typical in this regard,[22] and reflected their growing adherence to a European political role. The detailed European response was more difficult to achieve, partly because Kissinger's address had lacked specifics and partly because of divergent political viewpoints in Europe. Finally, in September, the Nine issued a joint statement responding to Kissinger's Atlantic Charter proposal. British Foreign Secretary Alec Douglas-Home observed that 'it was the first time that the Community as a whole had envisaged its joint relations with a third country',[23] but the statement did not contribute to a dialogue with the United States on Atlantic relations.

Perhaps with enough time and the proper conditions, it would have, but conditions soon worsened. The cause was the Middle East War of October 1973, which resulted in a temporary Arab oil embargo to the West and a permanent and sharp increase in prices. Again, American and European interests were at odds.[24] Recent history and differing degrees of oil dependency made the split hardly surprising, but political relations continued to

148

deteriorate. Movement towards a consolidated stand by oil-importing nations and towards a scheme for recycling petrodollars, thereby stabilising the international monetary system, progressed slowly and often acrimoniously,[25] and was accompanied by considerable bilateral activity. Nevertheless, Kissinger, in a speech to the National Press Club in February 1975, characterised the efforts of the International Energy Agency, which was formed in the aftermath of the Washington Energy Conference, as 'one of the major success stories of cooperation among industrialized democracies in the past decade'.[26] Whether that description is accurate or not, the basic tension in American-European relations has not been relieved.

The level of public conflict has varied, and undoubtedly will continue to do so. Relations have certainly not declined to the point where the Atlantic area cannot be considered a pluralistic security community. It was the early post-war relationship which was unnatural. The process of establishing a more balanced, and hopefully stable, relationship will be a lengthy one, dependent as much on internal developments in Europe and in the United States as on specific foreign policy stands, and is likely to involve ongoing adjustment rather than a fixed or static relationship.

Britain's role in this process up to now has not been extraordinary. While Britain finds the idea of being the spokesman for Europe appealing,[27] her partners have not been willing to defer to her and she, in turn, has not had the power to claim the position for herself. British leadership has, in fact, been evident on some issues, such as the European proposal on the recycling of petrodollars,[28] but the Community is not yet so unified that common positions can be developed on all major issues anyway.

Another view is to see the British as America's spokesman in the Common Market. The pejorative label for this role has been 'Trojan horse'. In a sense, the British have not been adverse to being a link between the Community and the United States. They and the Germans, for example, have been more disposed to see European development in an Atlantic context than have the French. British officials have constantly repeated the need for close European-American relations.[29] Moreover, the shaky progress of European cooperation has convinced some British that bilateral relations with the United States will continue to be important.[30]

This role, however, would seem to be illusory, despite the historical relationship. Whether there is a position for an American spokesman *within* the Community is far from clear. Even if there is, Britain's ability to fulfil that role seems doubtful, given her weakened conditions. For the very same reasons that an Anglo-American 'special relationship' on a global basis has disappeared, a scaled-down version in Europe holds no major attraction for the United States.

The future of Anglo-American political relations is limited in its possibilities. There is no basis for an independent political role for Britain in this direction. A fragmented Europe, with or without Britain, would perpetuate US domination. A politically unified Europe *might* play a more important role in the world, but the best the British could expect in such an arrangement is some influence, but not leadership. But if the decline in capabilities and in political unity in Britain continues, even influence will not be available.

Notes

[1] See George Liska, op. cit., p. 88.

[2] Ball, *The Discipline of Power* (Boston: Little, Brown and Co., 1968), p. 92.

[3] Quoted in Robert Kleiman, *Atlantic Crisis* (New York: W. W. Norton, 1964), p. 55.

[4] See John Newhouse, *De Gaulle and the Anglo-Saxons*, p. 199.

[5] This problem is examined in greater detail in Richard Neustadt, *Alliance Politics* (New York: Columbia University Press, 1970).

[6] See George Liska's discussion of the role of consultation in alliances, op. cit., p. 85.

[7] Kissinger, op. cit., p. 79.

[8] See pp. 101–2.

[9] *Christian Science Monitor* (20 October 1958).

[10] *The Sunday Times* (8 December 1963).

[11] All commentators agree that Macmillan's eloquent argument was critical at Nassau. See, for example, Arthur Schlesinger, Jr., *A Thousand Days* (Boston: Houghton-Mifflin, 1965), p. 737.

[12] On this, see Theodore Sorensen, *Kennedy* (New York: Harper and Row, 1965), p. 566; Kleiman, op. cit., p. 61; and Newhouse, *De Gaulle and the Anglo-Saxons*, p. 219.

[13] In addition to Macmillan's reply, cited previously, see David Ormsby-Gore's speech to the English-Speaking Union in Houston, Texas on 23 January 1963 (*The Times*, 24 January 1963).

[14] In fact, as noted previously, some officials in Washington were bitter that the British did not provide material assistance as well (see p. 100, note 5).

[15] *The Guardian* (10 October 1967).

[16] For example, see George Brown's speech to the House of Commons (16 November 1966).

[17] *The Economist* (14 October 1967), p. 120.

[18] Edward Heath spoke of the 'natural relationship' between Britain and the United States in 1973 (see *The Economist*, 27 January 1973, p. 14).

[19] *New York Times* (24 December 1971).

[20] *New York Times* (10 December 1971).

[21] *New York Times* (24 April 1973).

[22] *New York Times* (28 April 1973).

[23] *European Community* (November 1973), p. 3.

[24] For a fuller examination of this issue see Robert L. Pfaltzgraff, Jr, 'The Middle East Crisis: Implications for the European-American Relationship', paper presented at the 1974 Annual Meeting of the American Political Science Association, Chicago, Illinois.

[25] The split at the Washington Energy Conference in February 1974 illustrates this point.

[26] Henry Kissinger, 'Energy: The Necessity of Decision', *The Atlantic Community Quarterly*, vol. 13, no. 1 (Spring 1975), p. 7.

[27] See, for example, *The Economist* (27 January 1973), p. 14.

[28] *Washington Post* (15 January 1975).

[29] For examples from both parties, see 'Interview with Britain's Prime Minister Edward Heath', *US News and World Report* (21 December 1970), p. 24; and *Washington Post* (26 January 1975).

[30] See, for example, the speech by Foreign Secretary James Callaghan to the National Press Club on 21 May 1974.

14   Britain's Role

Britain, without an empire, without the capability to be an independent power, yet with a highly conscious desire to play a world role, has endeavoured to find an international alignment through which she could exert global influence. In one sense this search has been for a political role, an abstraction which has not been clearly defined but, rather, has been the product of historical tradition and self-perception.

Increasingly, however, the search for international alignments has been related to material needs, both economic and military. Such considerations have complicated Britain's search in a number of ways. First, the assessment of prospective coalitions has involved considering more factors. This has been especially significant since different options have offered differing attractions. Secondly, an accounting of abstract versus material benefits has not been easily accomplished. This has been true with respect to finding measures of comparison as well as to evaluating short versus long term impact. Thirdly, the change in the nature of Britain's needs and capabilities has lessened her bargaining strength in the international system. The search for a role has therefore involved more than choosing the most advantageous coalition: Britain has had also to gain the acceptance of others.

In previous chapters, functional components of coalition behaviour were examined. Beginning with a presentation of British needs and capabilities, attention was focused on the pattern of relations in each of the two international subsystems with respect to the three functional sectors. In this chapter, the patterns for the three sectors are compared and analysed. A starting point is made by analysing the set of nine propositions presented in chapter 1 (see pp. 8–9).

Evaluation

Proposition one, that the 'importance' of the link with Europe for Britain increased, while that of the connection with the United States decreased, lends itself to general evaluation. It may therefore be useful to consider the other eight first and then to return to this proposition as the basis for an overview.

In proposition two, it was suggested that the increase in 'importance' of Europe for Britain came first and most markedly in the economic sector. In these terms, the question of functional integration in the Anglo-European subsystem – whether in the progress of the process or in the establishment of background conditions for it – is raised. The significance of this sector is reinforced by the emphasis, both formal and practical, which the European Community has assigned to it. However, the original proposition was only partly substantiated. Of the three sectors involved, changes between 1958 and 1962 were, while not dramatic, most evident in the economic field. Indeed, by 1962 both trade and direct investment with the European Community had increased in 'importance' for the British. Moreover, the expectation was that this pattern would continue.

Regarding the second part of this proposition, which refers to overall magnitude, initial expectations were not entirely met. Thus there was a period of levelling-off in the mid-1960s with respect to both trade and investment. Moreover, the United States, rather than being supplanted, retained a high level of 'importance' for Britain, especially in the investment area.

At the same time, rather dramatic changes occurred in the other sectors of the Anglo-European subsystem. Contrary to proposition three, which is examined in greater detail below, a striking increase in 'importance' was observable in Anglo-European military relations. While this evolved later than the start of the new pattern in the economic sector, its overall impact was highly significant. Moreover, from the psychological perspective, the re-evaluation of the European subsystem as the basis for a British political role also represented a notable change.

With regard to economic integration in Anglo-European subsystem relations, changes in individual areas are revealing. The institutional barrier between the Common Market and Britain had a major impact in limiting transactions prior to the 1970s. Of course, in the trade field Britain had to compete in the face of tariff barriers. Perhaps more significantly, the Six increasingly concentrated their economic transactions within the Community. This development clearly demonstrated that Britain was not able to participate in the mainstream of economic integration in Europe. In this respect, she made only limited progress during the first half of the period under study. While the attraction was there, the actual benefits were not so impressive. Eventually, with membership assured, there was a sharp expansion of trade. At least from the British perspective, total trade figures would indicate a growing interdependence since membership.

The pattern of direct investment is less dramatic. Britain, which has always placed greater importance on foreign investment than have her European partners, has significantly increased her activity in the 1970s, but the total picture is still rather unbalanced. The amount of European investment in Britain has not increased to a high level, comparable to American investment, for example. This restraint, or hesitancy, would seem to suggest a conscious European effort to limit interdependence, largely due to a lack of confidence in the British economy.

With regard to policy interaction, the hypothesis is not fully substantiated, however. On the one hand, there was some early use of policy issues as a means of bargaining with the Europeans. Nevertheless, practical calculations rather than integrative pressures were decisive throughout. The significant changes in policy interaction, which came from the mid-1960s on, were the result of two factors: first, the shift in American international economic policy, and, secondly, British accession to the Common Market. In policy as in interactions, the institutional barrier has been a significant one for Britain, first *outside* and then *inside* the institutions. These changes came late rather than early.

Proposition three deals with the military sector and contends that the 'importance' of the United States remained well above that of Europe for the British, and that this sector showed the least change in 'importance' levels.

Both portions of this proposition were invalidated by the findings of this study. Rather, there has been a sharp increase in the 'importance' of the European subsystem for the British, in both policy orientation and transactions. This pattern has developed most markedly since the mid-1960s.

The military value of the link with the United States for Britain, while decreasing slightly, has remained high. Given America's military strength and her predominant role in NATO, this was to be expected. Moreover, as was suggested earlier, much of the cooperation and assistance undertaken was the product of agreements made during the first part of the period. This relationship, while remaining crucial to Britain's security, has involved a diminishing British input and, therefore, reduced influence.

As British leaders became aware of the impact of their reduced military capability, the need to reorder defence posture became apparent. Eventually this led to a growing concentration on European defence efforts, an emphasis that had been rejected for many years. Conscious policy shifts led the way and, while often related to the effort to join the Common Market, would have probably been undertaken even if there were no EEC. While the 'importance' of Anglo-European military relations has still not been fully developed, the belated recognition by the British that a European orientation is the most appropriate, or logical, gives this sector a significant future potential.

Contrary to the pattern in the economic sector, institutional structures have not been a major deterrent to military transactions. Rather, given the lack of a formal Community mechanism for dealing with the defence sector, the British were able to exert a degree of leadership in developing collaboration on weapons production. The institutional barriers proved to be an irritant at

155

times, but the limitations on greater progress in this sector were more the result of reluctance about supranationalism. Nevertheless, the 'importance' of transactions in Anglo-European military relations increased markedly.

The issue in which institutional factors had the greatest impact was the nuclear policy area. On the one hand, it was in this sector that the most elaborate formal agreements existed between the United States and Britain. These, in turn, provided a potential restraint on more widespread nuclear cooperation in the Anglo-European subsystem. More significant, however, was the lack of centralised decision-making authority in Europe. There is a general feeling that only a federal Europe could control and utilise a nuclear capability. While Edward Heath's proposal for an Anglo-French nuclear force to be held in trust for Europe remains a possibility, a federal Europe is clearly many years in the future.

The inapplicability of proposition three suggests the need to maintain flexibility in theorising about integration coalition behaviour. Predetermined categories of 'high' or 'low' politics may not correspond to actual political behaviour. To be sure, this case did not involve clearcut military integration. Nevertheless, the ability to shift emphasis if one sector seems cut off does not appear to be limited by functional divisions.

Proposition four states that the 'importance' of Europe for Britain in the political sector increased as her own economic and military capabilities decreased. In a broad sense, the period under study saw two trends which substantiate this notion. Chapter 13 suggested that the European subsystem was seen increasingly as the basis for a British political role. Similarly, the decline in both the economic and the military strength of the United Kingdom was discussed in chapters 2 and 8.

By 1962, the European connection was still only of low 'importance' to the British in the political sector. While there was concern with declining capabilities at this time, Britain's self-confidence remained high. The attitude during the first set of negotiations with the Common Market was that other options were available.

The nature of British weakness was more apparent by the time of the second try in 1967. There had been two more economic crises – in 1964 and in 1966 – and the pound sterling was devalued at the end of 1967. In the military sector, the Plowden Report had forecast a gloomy future for the British aircraft industry, the TSR2 had been cancelled, and the initial decision on withdrawal East of Suez had been made. Thus there was considerable emphasis in official statements on the political benefits of joining Europe. This was so despite the limited returns on material transactions within the Anglo-European subsystem up until this time.

From 1967 onwards, developments proceeded in the same direction.

Further admissions of British weakness were spelled out in early 1968 in the aftermath of devaluation. The emphasis on the political ties with Europe was greater by 1970 than at any time in the past. However, a variety of barriers, institutional and attitudinal, prevented this relationship from providing a totally satisfactory political role for the British. After 1972, the institutional barriers were removed, but it is still not clear whether attitudinal or psychological constraints have been resolved. This caveat, concerning the kind rather than the direction of a political role, does not invalidate the proposition which was concerned with comparative patterns rather than with the resolution of the search for a role, but it does question its relevance. This point will be discussed further.

With the previous limitation in mind, the correlation suggested in proposition four does seem to have been established. Some concepts from integration theory may be useful in trying to explain this development.

The distinction between positive and negative economic integration is pertinent. Britain's emphasis in the first few years of this period was on the minimisation of the impact of the Common Market. That is, while Britain did not want to participate, she was aware that exclusion might have damaging consequences. Therefore interest in the Community was primarily of a material nature. The free trade area proposal was motivated by this attitude, but even the first application stressed negative economic integration.

After the 1963 veto, there was no feeling of calamity, but rather a determination to carry on. However, as suggested above, the economic and military situation continued to deteriorate. With a renewed interest in Common Market membership in 1966, the attraction of positive economic integration was acknowledged. It was also increasingly realised that to achieve material benefits, participation in the political sector would also be required.

The interrelationship among sectors has been significant in two respects. First, the logic of cooperation has prevented a clear compartmentalisation of activities. 'Spillover', as the integration theorists describe it, is logical, even if not compelling or automatic. Therefore, to get the economic and military benefits they desired, the British have become willing to get involved in political activities as well. That this has not proceeded further does not detract from the interrelationship.

A second factor has increased the political attraction of Europe for the British. Where they once feared the evolution of a political union, that possibility now stands as one basis for a new British political role. By contrast, the attraction of a political role within the Anglo-American subsystem has declined.

The development of this pattern requires further explanation, and involves propositions five and six. To repeat, it was hypothesised that as British economic and military capability decreased, her bargaining ability, that is, her 'importance' to the United States and to the European Community, also decreased, and that the decline would be greater with respect to the United States than to the European Community.

By the latter half of the 1960s, Britain was no longer being offered a major political role within the relationship with the United States. The prerequisite for such a role previously was Britain's economic and military capability. Thus while the interrelationship of sectors was relevant to this subsystem, the process and timing of interaction were not the same as for Anglo-European relations.

An explanation for these contrasting patterns is seen in the differing nature of the two subsystems with respect to two factors: capabilities and objectives. The disparity between British and American capabilities was far more than that between Community and British ones. In this respect, the proposition from integration theory that a similarity in the size of the units is advantageous[1] seems to be relevant. As a second part of this point, the potential of the United States is developed to a far greater extent than that of the EEC. Expressed differently, the Community has not reached the same level of dynamic growth and may be more willing to consider changes which would help it to fulfil its potential. The inclusion of Britain in the Community *might* have the effect of providing a catalyst for the process. The assessment of that goes back to Riker's comments on establishing a 'winning coalition'.

As to objectives, it is clear that the two relationships, while fitting the definition of international subsystem, differ markedly. The basis for the Anglo-American alliance was strategic-diplomatic, 'high politics' in Raymond Aron's sense.[2] The relationship was a partnership. The purpose was to add capabilities together, not to engage in a conscious process of sector integration.

On the other hand, the original impetus for a conscious Anglo-European subsystem was economic. However, as many in Europe had long felt and as the British eventually recognised, the economic sector was linked to the military and political ones. The goal of integration was made explicit, with the hope that all sectors would eventually be included. Thus, amalgamation rather than addition has been the objective.[3]

As Britain's military and economic capabilities declined, she was less able to contribute to a partnership with the United States. This, in turn, undercut the basis for political cohesion. Meanwhile, by being willing to join in the political aspirations of the European movement, Britain enhanced her prospects for satisfying economic and military needs. Thus, Europe has acted as a 'core power' for Britain in a way that the United States has not.

Proposition seven was intended to examine bargaining strategy and suggested that overt demonstrations of commitment to Europe by the British were most intense during negotiations on membership.

In fact, the 'importance' of the European subsystem was not necessarily related to demonstrations of 'European-ness'. Demonstrations are gestures, and need not involve real changes in policy. Thus, by 1962, there had been no increase in the policy 'importance' of the European subsystem for Britain in either the economic or the military sector over that of 1958. This fact seems to have been a reflection of Britain's assessment of her own bargaining strength.

In line with this view, there was a sharp increase in the 'importance' in the military policy sector of the Anglo-European subsystem by 1967. Given the grounds for de Gaulle's first veto, it is possible to reach the conclusion that the British were using military policy as a means of demonstrating commitment to the European idea during the second attempt. At the same time, the change in the 'importance' of economic policy was slight.

By 1970, there was a large rise in the 'importance' of economic policy as well. The basis of de Gaulle's second veto, an insistence by the French on British agreement on monetary policy, and a split with the United States on trade policy, accounted for this shift. By this date, Britain's assessment of her bargaining strength had declined considerably. Thus the increases in 'importance' were largely the result of British policy shifts.

In an overview of the series of negotiations, two main processes are observable. First, the British underwent a learning process. Rather than merely utilising traditional diplomatic consultation or dramatic announcements, the British saw it necessary to incorporate certain policy changes even before membership was achieved. Moreover, it was recognised that such changes would have to encompass all sectors rather than just carefully selected convenient ones. Thus suspicions about the British commitment to Europe were less prevalent in the Community in 1970 than they had been in 1962, or even in 1967.

A second process developed with the decline of Britain's bargaining strength. The widening of the scope of demonstrations was somewhat self-fulfilling. Genuine changes in policy had to be instituted, thus increasing the urgency of achieving membership in the Common Market.

Interestingly, there has been a diminished willingness to engage in 'demonstrations' of European-ness since membership. In this respect, the British have been as concerned about 'national interests' within the Community as the French have. Indeed, the whole process of renegotiation was based on the premise that membership should be evaluated on a largely tangible national cost-benefit basis. This is certainly an approach far removed from the notion of making commitments to the idea of European unity, but it is a viewpoint which has, in fact, dominated the entire Community experience. That Britain should have felt compelled, and to some extent have been expected, to 'demonstrate her European-ness', highlights the difficult position she was in, trying to bargain for membership with an already established group rather than being an original member. Since entry, this constraint has been removed.

The eighth proposition was that after membership the 'importance' of British transactions with Europe would increase while there would be a corresponding decline in transactions with the United States. For foreign trade, the area in which the figures are most complete and Common Market structure most developed, the proposition is clearly confirmed. Being outside and then inside the Community's tariff barriers has made a substantial difference to British trade.

Direct investment figures are not adequate for evaluating the impact of membership. Prior trends indicate that British investment in Europe is, in fact, going up, but whether that has been affected by Community membership is not yet clear. Moreover, there is not yet evidence that Britain has attracted greatly increased investment from the Continent. Figures for a time period *after* the referendum are necessary to properly gauge the impact of British membership.

On the other hand, while Anglo-American trade has declined in relative 'importance', the level of American investment in the UK remains high. Similarly, there is no indication that British investment in the United States is diminishing.

From a theoretical perspective, these results would suggest that either foreign trade and overseas investment are measuring different aspects of economic relations or that there is a time-lag between the impact of the two indicators. The second possibility has already been suggested. The first warrants a brief additional comment. For a start, investment may be a more conscious measure of interdependence, in that a greater degree of control has generally been exerted over investment than over foreign trade. If that is correct, the gap between British and European activity in investment reflects differing assessments of the benefits of interdependence.

From another view, the attraction for investment may require a particular level, real or perceived, of economic viability;[4] that is, even political willingness to become interdependent may be prevented by the absence of a minimal level of economic confidence. Again, this approach might account for the difference in British and European investment levels.

Finally, there is the possibility that the impact of Anglo-European investment is distorted either by the dominant position of the United States in the investment sector or by the activity of multinational – the term non-national might also be appropriate – corporations. Anglo-European investment may be theoretically insignificant because there is so little opportunity for important policy impact. All three of these theoretical implications warrant further examination.

160

One other transaction, weapons acquisition, was measured. In this case, the proposition advanced seems insignificant. There has been no increase in collaborative prospects since 1973. Moreover, the United States is continuing its success in selling weapons systems to the Europeans, although not specifically to Britain.

The negative conclusion in this sector might be modified by two points. First, there is a lengthy lead-time in advanced technological projects. From that perspective, the period available in which to evaluate the impact of British membership in the EEC has been rather brief. Secondly, there were already several projects underway. Proceeding with those and evaluating the collaborative experiences of the past have been more important than any change resulting from British accession to the European Community.

Proposition nine, taken from Karl Kaiser, posits that overlapping subsystems in which a superpower participates interact in such a way as to foster the formation of subsystems excluding the superpower. One complication in evaluating this proposition concerns the numerous international links within the North Atlantic area. The two subsystems which are the focus of this study are not the only ones which affect this hypothesis. Therefore it is possible that countervailing patterns might either balance each other or obscure emerging trends. Thus an assessment of proposition nine must be tentative and subject to more sophisticated analysis. It is worth pursuing, however, because it has significant implications for further theorising and for the policy choices of the nations involved.

The first piece of evidence to consider is that, in all three sectors, the 'importance' of the United States for Britain has decreased, albeit sometimes only slightly. Moreover, these declines were noticeable in policy areas, suggesting a conscious pulling apart.

In the second place, much of the public discussion of developments within the North Atlantic area seems to accept the validity of this proposition. Thus both in Britain and on the Continent it is argued that only by joining together can Europe escape the domination of the United States. This is said to be the case with respect to both economic hegemony and American predominance in NATO.

By the same token, American reservations about European integration seem to be based largely on the fear of a split developing between the United States and a united Europe. Talk of a European 'Third Force' has subsided since the early 1960s with the realisation that integration in the defence sector is many years away. Concern with economic rivalry has persisted, however, and, in fact, has grown more acute since 1969.

Plans for either an Atlantic community or Atlantic partnership, such as the Kennedy Grand Design, represented specific efforts to forestall the split

161

envisioned by proposition nine. These proposals have not been successful to date and, indeed, the failure to reach agreement here might be seen as an indication of the tendency to diverge.

Yet, despite these considerations, there is a good deal of evidence to suggest that ties within the North Atlantic area remain strong. While the 'importance' of the United States for Britain has declined, it is still significant in both the military and the economic sectors. In addition, despite the internal disagreements of NATO, that organisation remains the basis for European defence. NATO's strength continues to rest primarily on American nuclear capability. Moreover, the European members of NATO oppose reductions in American troop strength in the alliance.

Yet it is not just in the military sector that the United States has maintained her presence. Indeed, in the economic field, interdependence within the entire North Atlantic area has increased as the result of growing American direct investment in Europe. While the Common Market provided an attraction to Britain, it also had the same effect on the United States. Rather than being excluded, the United States has dramatically increased its participation in this field.

An enlarged European Community might move away from the United States since it would, presumably, have a large measure of independent strength. Still, the international environment, other links of interaction, and the possibility of common interests, make the proposition uncertain.

Returning to proposition one, the anticipated trends were evident, but have not led to a resolution of Britain's search for a role. This has been a period of flux and turmoil. That should be a basic lesson for any student of international affairs. Moreover, for an observer of Britain's destiny, the evidence of historical irony is noteworthy. The British, who in the nineteenth and much of the twentieth century were so successful in exploiting their unique position, seem to be facing forces beyond their control. As is so clear, and has been for years, the old basis for Britain's prosperity, influence, or role is gone beyond reclamation. The effort to adjust – either by finding new resources for an old role or by pursuing a new, more manageable set of objectives – has been frustrated by innumerable factors.

The question of which role to pursue – as Dean Acheson suggested – seems to have been the wrong issue. If it were appropriate, we could analyse recent history either in terms of resources or of psychological factors, a study of British national character. Of course, both of those things have been done by numerous commentators and have been considered here. These factors are not wrong, but they necessarily leave an incomplete picture. The basic problem has been that the British have been trying to adjust to a world in which the rules and the relationships are changing so fast that the definition and

162

pursuit of a 'role' may be impossible. If the British dilemma is striking, it is, in fact, no different in kind than the situation faced by other international actors.

The drift and uncertainty faced by both the United States and the European Community in the mid-1970s as compared to ten or twenty years before are indisputable. In each of the functional areas examined, the system, or pattern of relations, is less secure, less stable than it once appeared to be. We can continually cite old systems which have broken down without being able to point to even the outline of their successors.

In this kind of international system, even a resolute and consistent British search would have been difficult. Inconsistency and uncertainty have made the task even more difficult.

Conclusion

Although recognising that a wide range of factors has complicated Britain's search for a role, this study has, nevertheless, identified a number of patterns that have been significant. Coalition behaviour has been more influenced by particular needs and capabilities than by abstract role-searching. This was so with respect to both alignment selection by a prospective member and admission or rejection of an applicant by an existing coalition.

Secondly, evaluations of alignment partners did indeed vary from one functional sector to another. The analytical decision to divide the substantive examination into economic, military, and political sections proved to be useful. Within each of these areas, the interaction of needs and capabilities was crucial to coalition behaviour. While the possibility of bargaining from one functional sector to another seems evident, and did in fact occur at times, it was certainly neither inevitable nor necessarily successful. Negotiating was most often on the basis of the lowest common denominator rather than an upgrading of common interests.[5]

Developments across these two subsystems during this period were not always directly correlated despite Britain's focal position. The choices were not either-or, but involved assessing a broad range of possibilities, some of them inherently contradictory, some of them complementary. Three factors can be seen to have accounted for this diversity.

First, as suggested above, the benefits of different alignments varied from one functional sector to the next. In the second place, choices outside the scope of these two subsystems were sometimes significant for the British. Thus, despite the explicit emphasis in British policy upon the North Atlantic area, the Commonwealth maintained a residual 'importance'. Thirdly, within the scope of the two subsystems under examination, other groupings or subsystems were also present, overlapping and interacting. To cite just a few institutional examples, these included NATO, OECD, GATT, and the International Monetary Fund.

From a different perspective, a pattern fundamental to this study was a decline in British capability, in both the economic and the military sectors. Without having to move to the level of individual motivation, it is clear that this trend was a major factor in determining the kind of coalition behaviour in which Britain engaged, that is, Britain's general need to reorder her foreign relations stemmed from the change in her own capabilities. Moreover, her bargaining power, the ability to *select* alignments, was also affected by the decline in economic and military strength. Thus, while the specific choices made by the British in this period were not predetermined, significant constraints were operating.

The preceding remarks should indicate Britain's complex position in her 'search for a role'. This, in turn, led to another pattern, indecisiveness by the British. Choices often seemed unclear and assessments of alternatives were difficult to make. In terms of policy output, the result was often ambivalence.

To speak of Britain doing this or not doing that is, of course, a description of aggregate political behaviour which to a considerable extent obscures the intricacies and motives of the political decision-making process. And, as the writers on bureaucratic politics have so aptly noted, the actions or decisions of a government are the product of a complex interaction of activities by organisations and individuals within that government. Moreover, the behaviour of individuals may also stem from various factors, some related to external reality and others to self-needs.

This is a study of aggregate behaviour, of Britain's search for a role. Without detailing the processes which produced that behaviour, it is still possible to put into perspective the dual character of the search. The examination of the foreign policy actions of a nation has the aspect of a national character study to it. On the one hand, the nation is attempting to deal with the external reality presented by the international system of which it is a part. In addition, however, self-perception and domestic needs, both material and psychological, influence policy and actions. The 'role' is as much defined, probably more so, by internal needs and perceptions as by the 'objective' reality of the world.

In a sense, this study disputes much of the rhetoric of recent British foreign relations. Indeed, what was missing was a coherent, unified policy thrust. Not merely victims of fate, the British did not make the best of the opportunities available to them.

In the first place, the realisation that their traditional role was no longer viable was stubbornly resisted. The decline in economic and military capability was for too long ignored. Even when the 'search for a role' became acknowledged policy, contradictions and hesitations remained. British leaders tried to avoid choosing, to keep all options open, and to maintain a myth of national sovereignty and independence.

An overestimation of British bargaining power was also prevalent. This was the product both of uncertain policy objectives and hesitation to accept the changing economic and military reality. As a result, numerous opportunities to improve the British position were lost.

Both major British political parties, countless civil servants, mass and elite opinion, and numerous individual leaders have participated in Britain's search for a new international role. The specific impact of any of these must be the subject of another level of analysis. Yet the product of their combined efforts, seen in the patterns of interaction discussed above, has not been a resolution of that search. By 1975, Britain, once the head of a worldwide empire, once an acknowledged great power, has re-adjusted her ambitions, but has not yet satisfied them.

Notes

[1] Haas and Schmitter, op. cit., p. 266.

[2] Raymond Aron, *Peace and War* (Garden City: Doubleday, 1966), p.87.

[3] Amalgamation can, of course, take different forms. The minimum is negative economic integration, the maximum, political union.

[4] For investment in an underdeveloped nation, an ability to exercise influence or control might be substituted for an evaluation of economic strength.

[5] For a discussion of bargaining within the Community see Leon Lindberg, 'Decision-Making and Integration in the European Community', *International Organization*, vol. 19, no. 1 (Winter 1965).

Index

Some references may be to footnote indices; if the subject cannot be found on the page quoted, reference should be made to the notes at the end of the chapter for a lead.

Kennedy, President J. F. 39, 46, 102, 144–5
Kennedy Round 39, 46
Kissinger, Dr Henry 103, 135, 143, 148–9

Labour's (political) views *see* Wilson, (James) Harold
Labour relations 21, 22, 23
Layton, Christopher 72
Lend-lease 16
London, City of, as financial capital 15

MacMahon Act (US – 1946) 101
Macmillan, Harold 18, 27, 87–8, 92, 101, 106, 143–5
Macrae, Norman 21, 26
McNamara, Robert 92, 102, 114, 144
Malaysia 91
Manila Conference (1966) 100
Manpower for defence 82
Markets, the search for new 37–8
Martin, L. W. 79, 85, 94, 97
Mason, Roy 92
Migration levels 31
Military Assistance Programme (MAP), termination of 111, 114
Military policy, UK's:
  Britain and Europe 87–95; regional policy 87–92; nuclear relations 92–5
  Britain and United States 99–106; global co-operation 99–101; nuclear relations 101–5; special relationship 105–6
  see also Defence policy
Mills Trade Bill (US – 1970) 47
Mirage aircraft 118, 124
Missiles: projects cancelled 84; purchases 111–13
Monetary Union 32, 38, 42–3, 135; *see also* International Monetary Union
Monnet, Jean 131
Multilateral Force (MLF) 89, 103–4, 146
Multinational corporations 74
Multi-role combat aircraft (MRCA) 119
Mutton, New Zealand 15

NAFTA 46–7
Nassau (1962) 101, 103–4, 144–5
National Institute of Economic and Social Research 62, 64
National Service, ending of 82
National unity, need to develop a sense of 65
NATO 70, 80, 82, 87–94, 99, 101, 103, 105, 116, 119, 124, 146, 155, 161–2; Labour

Government view of 89, 91–2; Conservative view of 91
Newhouse, John 95, 97
New York Times, The 147
New Zealand 15, 39, 92
Nixon, President R. M. 42, 46–8, 51, 147–8
North Sea oil 65
Nuclear: Non-Proliferation Treaty 100; relations: Britain and Europe 92–5; Britain and United States 101–5
Nye, Joseph 3, 6

OECD 17, 45
OEEC 45
Oil: crisis 42, 135–6, 148; trade deficit on 65
Overseas investment, direct 67–74

Paris Summit Conference: (1972) 135; (1974) 136
Per capita income 31
Persian Gulf 100
Petrodollars 148
Pinder, John 27
Plowden Report (1965) 115, 117, 122, 123, 156
Polaris missiles 102–5, 110–11, 126, 145
Political relations, UK's:
  Anglo-European 131–8; British negotiations with EEC 131–5; Britain within EEC 135–8
  Anglo-American 141–50; background conditions 142; special relationship 143–50
Pompidou, President Georges 134
Poseidon 104
Pound *see* Sterling system
Preferential trading 37–40
Propositions for this study *see under* Analysis
Protectionism 47

Raw materials, UK's need to import 16
Referendum issues 137–8
Regional policy (military) 87–92; political goals of 30–2, 38
Report on Defence (White Paper – 1960) 116
Riker, William 4, 158
Rippon, Geoffrey 41
Rogers, Secretary of State 148
Role of Britain 153–65; evaluation 153–163; conclusion 163–5

Rolls Royce, Ltd. 18, 117
Rusk, Dean 142

SALT 95, 100–1
Sea-Dart project 117
SEATO 99–100
Servan-Schreiber, J.-J. 71, 73
Singapore 91–2
Skybolt missile 101–5, 143–5
Smithsonian Conference (1971) 51
Social Contract 23
Sovereignty, question of loss of 138
Soviet nuclear power 95
Space projects 118, 121
Special relationship (with US) *see* United
   States, special relationship with
'Stagflation' 23
Sterling system 28, 40–1, 50, 147
Strikes 21–3
Suez: crisis (1956) 141, 143; role east of
   80–1, 89–92, 100, 105, 146–7, 156
Summit Conferences *see* Copenhagen;
   Hague; Manila; Nassau; Paris (2)
Sugar problems 39–40
Sunday Times, The 100

Technology 72–4, 119–23
Third Force, idea of European 9
Thor missiles 101
Times, The 79, 133
Trade:
   deficits 62–3; Expansion Act (US – 1962)
      39, 46; UK need for good 15, 32
   UK policy: and Europe 37–40; and
      United States 45–8
   see also Direct overseas investment;
      Foreign trade
Treaty of Rome 38, 132; Art. 108 41
Training programmes, ECSC 30

TSR2 project 115, 117, 156

U–2 incident 144
UK economy:
   history and capabilities 15–25: introduc-
      tion 15–16; changing capabilities 16–25
   integration and adjustment 27–38: sum-
      mary 32–3
   policy, Britain and Europe 37–43: trade
      policy 37–40; international monetary
      policy 40–3
   policy, Britain and the United States 45–
      51: trade policy 45–8; international
      monetary policy 48–51
UK, negotiations with EEC 131–5; *see also*
   Role of Britain
Under-developed areas of the six 30
Unemployment rate 31
Unilever, Ltd. 18
United Nations, Security Council of 99
United States: military sales to Britain
   110–11; special relationship with 1, 8,
   102, 105–6, 143–50; trade with 37
Upper Clyde Shipbuilders, Ltd. 18

Wage restraint policy *see* Social Contract
Watkinson, Harold 102
Weapons acquisition problem 85, 109–26,
   161: Britain–United States 110–16;
   Britain–Europe 116–23; interaction
   123–6
Werner Report 42
Western European Union (WEU) 80, 82,
   88, 116
Westlands, Ltd. 119
Wilson, (James) Harold 21–2, 28, 33, 70,
   93–4, 133–4, 137–8, 146

YF–16 aircraft 124

The Author

Dr Boyd took his Ph.D. at the University of Pennsylvania in 1971 and is now Assistant Professor of Political Science at the University of Baltimore.